Welcome

For many of us, the Victorians are the ultimate exemplars of strait-laced normality. But have you ever thought about the fact that they were, well... more than just a little bit weird? In reality, Victorian Britain was a seething cauldron of the strange. Folkloric beliefs from all over the Empire on which the sun never set collided head-on with the Victorian industrial complex, which was busily churning out almost magical technologies like radio, photography and electricity – as well as deadly wallpaper that would make you see ghosts, killer mascara, and knock-out drugs. Factory owners behaved like feudal barons, while the poor indulged their violent kicks for a penny a pop, the upper and middle classes hid their vices behind closed doors and strict manners, and the supernatural haunted the popular imagination. Lift the lid on this bizarre era and learn just how weird the Victorians really were.

CONTENTS

Society & Culture

14 FREAKY FASCINATIONS
The Victorians were fascinated by oddities, from exotic creatures to – sadly – unusual people

22 A SOUR NOTE: VINEGAR VALENTINES
Valentines cards weren't just for lovers: in the Victorian era, some were written with insults in mind

24 A VERY VICTORIAN CHRISTMAS
The Victorian Christmas set the template for our own, but we don't practice these bizarre festive traditions

28 ALL THE WORLD IN A BOX
The Victorian vogue for curiosity cabinets saw all sorts of strange objects displayed in family parlours

30 NO HOLDS BARRED: THE SWEET SCIENCE OF BAREKNUCKLE BOXING
Victorian sport could be brutal, and none more so than boxing when the gloves were off

36 BABY FARMERS
For overcrowded families, there were women to take on unwanted children – for a very heavy price

38 SUN, SEA AND SOCIAL BREAKDOWN
When the Victorian masses visited the seaside, their strict morality might slacken...

44 WAKES WEEK
An old church tradition was transformed into a way for factory workers to take a holiday

46 IN FOR A PENNY
The very poorest had little access to fun and games, apart from those that cost a penny

50 TURN TO THE WALL, GIRL!
Victorian servants were expected to follow some bizarre etiquette customs at work

52 CONSPICUOUS CONSUMPTION
For romantic Victorians, the ideal beauty standard was the distinctive look of tuberculosis

56 MANNERS MAKETH (WO)MAN
A day in the very polite society of the average upper class Victorian lady

58 MORAL OUTRAGE
Victorian attitudes to sex and sexuality weren't as simple as they first appeared

Contents

Religion & Belief

64 HIGH CHURCH, LOW CHURCH
Victorian Christianity was a tale of two church styles: rich and ritualistic or the simplicity of holy poverty

68 MUSCULAR CHRISTIANITY
The strange Victorian movement for men that saw faith allied with physical prowess and athleticism

70 SUPERSTITIONS, OMENS AND HAUNTINGS
In popular belief, the Victorian world was fraught with supernatural powers, entities and creatures

76 SPRING-HEELED JACK
A famous demon stalked – and sprang – through the streets of Victorian London

78 VICTORIAN OCCULT
An in-depth look at the Victorian longing to connect with the spiritual world of life after death

88 THE DEVIL'S FOOTPRINTS
A strange phenomenon that plagued the residents of a small town in the south of England

90 THE OCCULT REVIVAL
The Victorian magicians who believed they were on the trail of ancient sorcery and sacred power

96 MODEL VILLAGES AND TEMPERANCE TOWNS
How factory owners exerted moral control through the provision of workers' housing in new towns

Industry & Invention

102 THE SPIRIT OF INVENTION
Some of the Victorian era's most world-changing inventions and how they transformed society

110 SCHEELE'S GREEN: THE DYE OF DEATH
The invention of a vivid green dye for wallpaper soon brought home more than the Victorians bargained for

112 TWILIGHT SLEEP
The groundbreaking but strange procedure that was a prelude to modern anaesthesia

114 THE EYE OF THE BEHOLDER
If you think TikTok beauty fads are weird, try these Victorian ones on for (corseted) size

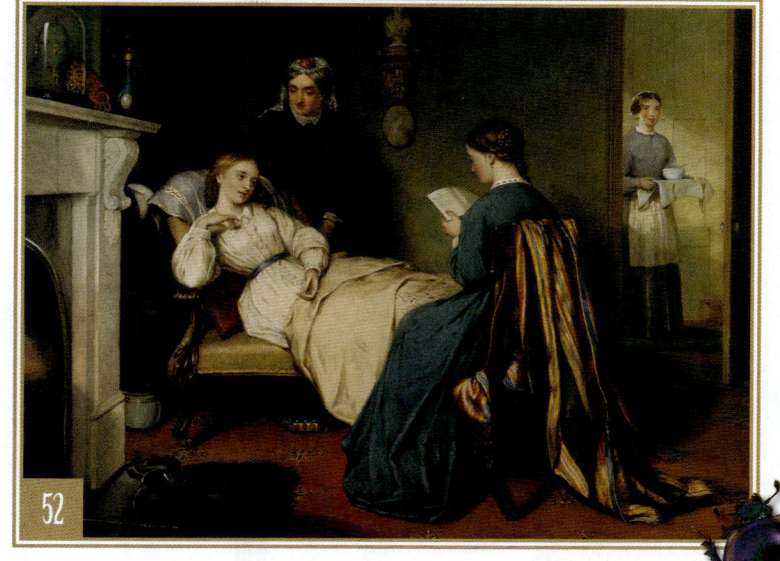
52

30

118 THE GOLDEN AGE OF TAXIDERMY
The Victorian era's fascination with the exotic and discovery of new chemical processes created a boom in dead displays

120 CSI WHITECHAPEL: VICTORIAN FORENSICS
With Jack the Ripper on the streets, Victorian detectives needed new ways to investigate murders

126 THE EVERLASTING STAIRCASE
For prisoners in Victorian gaols, the ultimate punishment was pointless and exhausting labour

128 THE CRYSTAL PALACE
Scene of Victorian Britain's most dazzling showcase, visit the imperial expedition of British invention and progress

THE WEIRD WORLD OF THE VICTORIANS

Written by Jack Griffiths

Alongside the forward leaps in science and technology, the Victorian era also had many quirky customs and traditions that formed an eccentric culture

The Weird World Of The Victorians

Queen Victoria's 63-year reign oversaw a period of upheaval with expansion of the empire, technological advancements and aspects of culture we can still see today

Introduction

The Victorian era was a time of progress. The Industrial Revolution was in full flow with railways covering the countryside and cities rapidly expanding and modernising. The British Empire grew significantly – into the largest the world had ever seen – and became known as "the empire on which the sun never sets". The understanding and use of medicine developed, society morphed from predominantly rural communities to more heavily concentrated populations dwelling in larger urban areas, and the first ideas of biological evolution took form. The period even saw the first telephones and the analytical engine, a mechanical calculator that was a distant ancestor of the modern computer. Away from technology, industry and military conquest though, the Victorians were a curious lot, partial to a bit of quirky weirdness in their culture and social lives. From hair jewellery to seaweed scrapbooking and even elephant deliveries, welcome to the weird world of the Victorians...

The developments in science and technology and the conditions in which people lived, shaped Victorian culture. An enduring image of Victorian Britain is that of the workhouse. Brought to life through the likes of *Oliver Twist*, families, many who had moved from the country to the cities, worked long, tough hours for little reward. This era witnessed the birth of British cities as we know them today. For example, Bradford and Glasgow grew eight times their size in 50 years, and Preston multiplied by six. Britain's urban population boomed. 80 per cent of Britons lived in the countryside in 1750. Within 100 years, this number had reduced to 20 per cent. Overall, Britain's population increased from around 27 million in 1851 to just over 41 million in 1900 and, as a nation, it was described as 'the workshop of the world'. British cities weren't just all smog and machinery though. Pleasure gardens and public parks with promenades and bandstands offered the public a place to unwind – if you could afford the time or money to enjoy them.

More than three-quarters of the population were working class, for whom life was tough in the growing and overcrowded cities, striving to make ends meet on a typical salary of less than £100 a year. Reform and action gradually improved living conditions but it was a long slog in the slums with high death rates and cholera, smallpox and tuberculosis epidemics. As a result, people turned their attention to weird and wonderful street games, interesting food choices or even lives of crime to forget about the factory or threat of the workhouse.

Britain was modernising, fast, and the world seemingly grew smaller too. The expansion of the railroads allowed more and more Victorians to enjoy the pleasures of seaside towns, many of which became popular holiday resorts for city folks who enjoyed their long piers jutting out to sea and penny arcades. Pioneers like engineer Isambard Kingdom Brunel built steam-powered shipping that could cross the Atlantic to the Americas and then

London became a bustling metropolis and the centre of an empire but its hard-working residents knew how to enjoy themselves, in often quirky ways

all the way down under to Australia. As well as a showcase of technical prowess, it allowed Britain to be a major player in international trade and to be at the forefront of the coming together of different cultures, worldwide. And to demonstrate gunboat diplomacy when military force was required too. From the 1830s onwards, locomotives delivered cargo and passengers across the country as 2,441 miles (3,920km) of train tracks criss-crossed Britain by 1845. This grew to 18,680 miles (30,063km) by

> **"2,441 MILES OF TRAIN TRACKS CRISS-CROSSED BRITAIN BY 1845"**

1900, with trains now chugging around the nation at speeds of more than 70 miles per hour (113km/h). It wasn't just above ground either; the London Underground opened in 1863. The first telegraph systems were established and cables were laid underwater in the Channel in the 1850s and the Atlantic in 1866, facilitating communication with France and the USA, respectively.

Britain only became entangled in one European land-based war in the era (the Crimean War), but nevertheless readied itself for any invading force. The Palmerston Forts of the coast of Portsmouth and Plymouth were built in the 1850s to protect the two key ports from potential attack, particularly the threat of the French Navy. The dark circle forts remain there to this day, and can be seen from the coast, marooned and alone, a relic of long-gone military might. Dark and foreboding, these forts signify a movement to dispense of Romanesque and classical architecture and replace it with brooding Gothic. The Houses of Parliament were rebuilt in 1835 in this style, rather than going down the classical route like the White House in Washington DC. The revival of the Gothic style can also be seen at St Pancras Railway Station, several buildings at the University of Oxford, and Tower Bridge.

These new aesthetics helped Britain's high streets to do roaring trade, with department stores the new way to shop. In 1849, Harrods shifted from a grocery and tea shop to a large department store and other retailers followed suit, including the now luxury chain Harvey Nichols. The stores were staffed by shop assistants, sometimes working 15-hour shifts, six days a week. These assistants could expect the unexpected – William Whiteley, who founded the shopping centre of the same name – boasted that on the shelves "would be everything from a pin to an elephant". After his bluff was called, an elephant was promptly delivered to the naysayer's house. The new department stores were a world away from the street markets and bazaars of old. Bon Marché employed a pneumatic tube system to transfer cash around the building, while Gamages was known to sell chimpanzees and porcupines – in case you always wanted one. This wasn't the only department store that included animals as part of the experience.

The Weird World Of The Victorians

Astley's Amphitheatre wowed Londoners with tricks, shows and dramas on horseback as well as staples like jugglers, clowns and acrobats

Queen Victoria was known as the 'grandmother of Europe' as Victorian influence spread far and wide, her name lent to foreign cities and landmarks

Cities became crowded places. A vibrant culture was a must to try and forget about long hours at workhouses and the squalor of the slums

THE CORONATION OF QUEEN VICTORIA

Victoria had an incredible influence over society during her 63 year reign

The Victorian era is synonymous with the reign of Queen Victoria. Her rule encompassed the vast majority of the period and oversaw industrial advancement and colonial expansion. She became queen while still a teenager after the death of her uncle, William IV, in 1837. Crowned in Westminster Abbey in a five-hour ceremony, it reportedly took longer than necessary due to a lack of rehearsal. When the royal party finally emerged, almost half a million people lined London's streets on 28 June 1838.

Lord Melbourne was the prime minister when Victoria was crowned and she would work with many over long era, including the long-serving Disraeli and Gladstone, but from a more distant standpoint than her predecessors. Victoria was the first British monarch to ride a train, the first to have her profile on an adhesive public postage stamp and the first to have a telephone in a royal palace.

She married Prince Albert three years after her coronation, and she would go on to have nine children with him. In 1845, she purchased Osborne House on the Isle of Wight, one of her favourite residences, and Balmoral also came under royal management under Victoria, the Scottish Highlands reminding Albert of his German heritage.

Victoria was only 18 when she was crowned. Her 63-year-reign is second to only Queen Elizabeth II on the list of the longest-serving British monarchs

---

Flamingos lived atop Derry and Toms in a roof garden, while Chiesmans went even further with elephants and lions on show.

For those that couldn't afford the fine ornaments on sale in these department stores, there was always hair jewellery. Exactly what it says on the tin, hair was woven into bracelets, rings and necklaces as a show of love or friendship. Additionally, the hair was sometimes cut off dead relatives and kept as a memory. The hair was twisted with pins in the same way as a wig into the desired design including bows, chains and beads.

Christianity was the leading religion in Victorian Britain, with numbers of other faiths increased by immigration into the British Isles from around the empire. The progress of science and Darwin's theory of evolution questioned the importance and status of religion and the philosophies of agnosticism and atheism grew. Sunday was still a holy day and a day of rest. However, with a day off to do what they wanted, workers often didn't take the 'rest' part to heart, with the birth of 'Saint Monday' – an unproductive or even absent day of work after living the high life the day before.

The Victorians had a fascination with Spiritualism. Contacting the dead at a séance was undertaken at home or at a crowded venue. Ouija boards (then called 'talking boards') were commonly used and speaking to lost souls intrigued the Victorians who were witnessing unprecedented technological and scientific advances – anything seemed possible, even talking to the dead. Spiritualism became a core part of Victorian culture with a number of societies and associations and began to make inroads on a population that was growing more sceptical of organised religion after more answers were being provided by science. Death played a big part in culture. Medicine advanced greatly from a focus on prayers, laxatives and even leeches to the first antiseptics, vaccines and anaesthetics. However, life expectancy was still only in the 40s so illness and funerals were a frequent occurrence. Strangely, families often posed for photographs with the dead to commemorate them, while wax death masks were made to put onto the faces of dead bodies.

Victorian culture was showcased at The Great Exhibition of 1851, a grand event that took place in Hyde Park, at the huge glass Crystal Palace. It was the brainchild of Prince Albert. Six million people attended the seminal event that had more than 100,000 exhibits. The vast majority of people could never travel abroad for leisure so the exhibition enabled them to see artefacts from across the world, including a Roman villa, a replica 15 metre (50 feet) statue of Ramesses II from an ancient Egyptian temple, Abu Simbel, and the Koh-I-Noor diamond, a jewel that is now part of the British Crown Jewels. Not to be outdone, Earl's Court put on a number of

Introduction

It wasn't just London that grew. Blackpool's famous tower opened in 1894, a symbol of the seaside as a place of leisure for Victorians

shows in including *Buffalo Bill's Wild West show*, and the Olympia exhibition centre showcased 'Venice in London', an imitation of the famous Italian city complete with gondolas and canals. One attendee was he of elephant delivery fame, William Whiteley. Hooked on what he witnessed, he went on to create the Whiteleys shopping centre.

Culture could also be found in theatres – Victorians loved a melodrama – but also in music halls where folk music was played and was accessible for the working class. Prince Albert also posthumously lent his name to the Royal Albert Hall, opened in 1871 in London in the style of a Roman Amphitheatre to showcase the latest in art and science. An increase in literacy rates meant many people could get their news from newspapers and enjoy novels, such as those of Charles Dickens, Lewis Carroll's *Alice in Wonderland* and Robert Louis Stevenson's *Treasure Island*. Many foodstuffs, which we know and love today, have their origins in the period. Curry was huge to middle and upper-class Victorians, the Queen herself particularly fond of the dish. Popular modern cakes were also introduced in this period. The humble Battenberg was first tasted, as was, of course, the Victoria sponge.

After the gin crazes of the 18th century, where dangerous amounts of drinking took place in the streets of London, gin palaces were created as a safer place to drink. Gin was often cheaper than beer but these palaces still had the funds to be lit by gas lighting and the décor was much more appealing for many than the pubs – which were often just the front rooms of people's houses, hence the name 'public house'. As well as their aesthetic differences, pubs tended to encourage their visitors to sit down and also to eat, while gin palaces were stand up and exclusively drinking affairs. Eventually, pubs began to emulate the decoration of the gin palaces, with fancy mirrors and long wooden bars. .

While drinking remained a common pastime, the temperance movements also put forward the ideas of teetotalism. They saw sobriety as a way of progressing the role and standing of the working class, without the reputation of drunkenness. They were dismayed at the idea of a gin palace, claiming that the appealing architecture masked the sin of drinking. Whether you were a drinker or not, dancing was popular in Victorian Britain. From grand ballrooms to pubs, live bands were commonplace. In the summer, fairs and pleasure gardens hosted live music from orchestras to

> "VICTORIANS LOVED A GOOD HOUSE PLANT, WITH FERN THE KING OF THE PREFERRED FLORA"

brass bands. London's Laurent's Casino wasn't for gamblers, instead it was a converted exhibition hall that was so popular that imitators were opened in Manchester, Sheffield and Leeds.

If the allure of vibrant nightlife didn't attract you, how about collecting plants? Victorians loved a good house plant, with fern the king of the preferred flora. It wasn't just the plant itself, ferns were drawn in art, mentioned in literature and its image was featured on numerous items around the Victorian house. Fern hunting was also a common hobby, with expeditions to Britain's fern hotbed, Devon, to restock the house's fernery. The Victorians really liked plants. Case in point, seaweed books. Seaweed scrapbooking was the pasting and pressing of seaweed onto paper to create elaborate designs. Seaweed hunters would frequent Britain's beaches to claim a haul of the algae to add into their books but also to publish guides on the best methods and types of seaweed scrapbooking.

The Victorians also had a fondness for wild animals and the expansion of the empire enabled the importation of exotic beasts into Britain. The first three public zoos are considered to be in Vienna,

The Great Exhibition of 1851, held in the huge Crystal Palace, showcased Victorian culture, as well as the plunders of empire

Madrid and Paris in the last years of the 18th century. London hosted a private scientific zoo from 1828 but the first public zoos in the British Isles were in Dublin in 1831, Brighton in 1832 and Liverpool the following year. London Zoo finally opened to the public in 1847, and, within three years, boasted the first hippopotamus enclosure in Europe.

Those who didn't have the funds to travel could catch a glimpse of a tiger or an elephant at one of the travelling menageries, where wagonloads of exotic animals pitched up at towns to wow crowds around the nation. If you were that enamoured by the animals on show, you could buy one to take home. These weren't just your modern household pets, you could buy a tiger or a snake if you so wished from one of London's 118 wild animal dealers or the many others in other British cities. Or, if you didn't have the money, you may spot one walking down the street. There are reports of tigers escaping captivity and taking a stroll through London. In 1857, a tiger escaped and picked up a boy, John Wade, in its mouth. The animal trader Charles Jamrach managed to free the boy, who survived, by snatching Wade out from the tiger's jaws. The incident is now memorialised in a statue at Tobacco Dock, Wapping. Jamrach was sued by Wade's parents for the incident but still continued his trade, his collection ranging from armadillos to zebras.

Poorer families also often kept birds as pets such as blackbirds and thrushes, housed in cages around and outside their homes. Rabbits and guinea pigs also started to become household pets at this time. Cats were still perceived largely as working animals whose job it was to control household pests, but this would shift by the end of the period. The cats outperformed hedgehogs, who were also bizarrely kept and tasked with keeping kitchens clear of insects. Despite the abundance of wild animals on show, canines were still top dog. The Kennel Club was founded in 1873, playing a crucial role in establishing breeding standards and shaping dog shows. Queen Victoria owned a number of different breeds of dogs. Collies were likely her favourite, she had more than 80! Victorians were so fond of their pets that they even had pet cemeteries, one of which remains in Hyde Park, London.

Talking about cemeteries, a curious Victorian pastime was the idea of cemetery picnics. More popular in the USA than in Britain, in the absence of public parks, graveyards filled in as a place for a quiet lunch with friends and family, amongst the dead. Taxidermy was also popular in the Victorian age. Stuffed animals were featured in elaborate scenes, including weddings, schools and ice-skating, which could be considered in bad taste now or just a bit weird. More simply, a pet would often be stuffed and displayed in the house so it would stay with the family in some capacity.

Circuses were also popular. Philip Astley is considered the 'father of the modern circus'. Along with his wife, Patty, he set up a riding school that included daring tricks and comical stories undertaken on horseback around a ring. From here, the staple circus attractions were introduced including acrobats, jugglers and clowns. His success, and the burning down of his initial location, enabled him to move to a larger venue called Astley's Royal Amphitheatre. After Astley's death, the business was taken over by one of the performers who changed the focus to equestrian plays with the horseback escapades. Some circus rings were filled with water for aquatic shows and, even with the added complexity of water shows, they travelled to locations across Britain so as many as possible could witness the wonders of the circus. When a circus rolled into town, you knew about it. Its arrival was announced with a mass parade of performers, bands, horses and wagons. Victorians also enjoyed early funfairs and the first steam-powered carousels. These merry-go-rounds had the same look as modern versions with flying animals to ride upon.

Both weird and wonderful, the quirkiness of the Victorian era's culture continues to fascinate with some of its aspects still evident in today's society but some best left as strange relics of the past.

⤜ EXPANDING THE EMPIRE ⤛

British influence reached new heights during the Victorian era

Despite losing the Thirteen Colonies after the American Revolutionary War in 1783, the British Empire still commanded a huge area. Boosted by the fall of Napoleonic France in 1815, Britain became the leading global power. The Indian Subcontinent, Australasia and many Caribbean islands still flew the Union Flag, as did many regions in Africa. In fact, the empire only expanded over the 100 year period from 1815-1914, with 10 million square miles (16 million square kilometres) and more than 400 million people now within the empire's boundaries, which comprised one fifth of the land on Earth. This period is known as the second British Empire and it continued to maintain its borders and global influence.

The empire was boosted by the opening of the Suez Canal in 1869, substantially reducing travel time to many territories. So Britain could more effectively coordinate its rule, areas such as Canada, Australia, New Zealand and South Africa were allowed to have 'responsible self-government' by the middle of the century. British power and influence was so complete that this era is sometimes known as 'Pax Britannica', which is Latin for 'British Peace' and a reference to when the Roman Empire was at its height under 'Pax Romana'.

At the end of the Victorian period, the British Empire had nearly a quarter of the world's population under its rule

Society & Culture

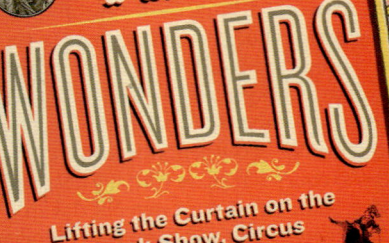

Contents

Society & Culture

14 Freaky fascinations
22 A sour note: Vinegar valentines
24 A very Victorian Christmas
28 All the world in a box
30 No holds barred: The sweet science of bareknuckle boxing
36 Baby farmers
38 Sun, sea and social breakdown
44 Wakes week
46 In for a penny
50 Turn to the wall, girl!
52 Conspicuous consumption
56 Manners maketh (wo)man
58 Moral outrage

Society & Culture

FREAKY FA

LIFTING THE LID ON THE WEIRD AND WONDERFUL

Freaky Fascinations

SCINATIONS

Written by David J Williamson

WORLD THAT WAS THE VICTORIAN FREAK SHOW

Society & Culture

The very idea of a freak show may be completely alien to our modern way of thinking, but the origins of this love affair with the unusual side of nature goes back hundreds, if not thousands of years. It ranges from Goliath in the *Old Testament* to the depictions of impish dwarfs that adorned the pottery and stonework of ancient Greece and Rome, and on to the underground dwellers of Norse and Germanic mythology who would both trick and curse unsuspecting humans for pleasure or revenge. Indeed, the original meaning of the word 'freak' is that of a sudden change, a trick or a prank, and as we shall see there is more than a little truth in this.

For dwarfs in particular it was to be the royal houses of Europe that were to set the tone for how they and other people of natural difference were to be viewed. Kings and queens - from Spain to Poland to England - counted among their households at least one dwarf. It was thought that their bodies made them almost mythical creatures, born out of the supernatural, that would bring good fortune.

Most notable in England was Jeffrey Hudson, court dwarf to Henrietta Maria, queen of the doomed Charles I. Pampered and protected by the queen, he rose from a poor background to be an entertaining addition to the Stuart court. But with this charmed lifestyle came a price, and many questions. Was it just good fortune that made his diminutive size so appealing to the queen and her court? Was his entertaining and witty character much larger than his physical presence? Or did his size make him nothing more than an amusing pet just like the other exotic animals with which Maria adorned her apartments?

The fascination with physical difference wasn't just a privileged entertainment. Between the 16th and 18th centuries travelling displays of human 'monstrosities' zig-zagged across Europe to entertain and amaze. Although saved from this existence, Jeffrey Hudson was in many ways just as much on display.

Annie Jones Elliot (1865-1902) also known as 'The Bearded Lady', toured with the showman PT Barnum as a circus attraction

By the early years of the 19th century individuals such as the dwarfish Józef Boruwłaski were thrilling the aristocratic courts of Europe. Literally at the other end of the scale, the Englishman Daniel Lambert - weighing in at over 52 stones - found his way into a nation's hearts through pamphlets and promotion to symbolise the very essence and physical power of the blossoming British Empire. This was a new kind of self-preservation and self-promotion; the freaks of nature taking control of their own exhibition. Not for them the lowliness of the travelling show. They were to 'receive' visitors in expensive and comfortable rooms, their 'appearances' more a private meeting, using the morbid interest in their unusual physiques to their own advantage both financially and for controlling how they wished to be seen by the world.

> "IT IS A WAY OF MAKING A LIVING, AND WE ARE VERY GRATEFUL"

As the 19th century dawned, for the freak shows the questioning minds of the medical and scientific communities were, not surprisingly, never far away. The word 'scientist' had not yet been used, nor for that matter had 'disability', but for many of the promoters of exhibitions of freaks in the early Victorian era, medical and scientific interest in their performers was a sure-fire way of grabbing the attention of the press and the public at large.

In 1829 the Egyptian Hall in Piccadilly, London, hosted a remarkable event. Having exhibited in a number of towns and cities in the USA, conjoined twins Chang and Eng astonished, delighted and intrigued their audiences in a masterful display of skill and spectacle. Even though joined at their upper body they were still able to perform somersaults and other acrobatics, as well as batting a shuttlecock between them at lightning speed. They were billed as the Siamese Twins (after their birthplace of Siam, or modern Thailand) - an expression that soon found its way into general usage to describe conjoined twins right up to the present day.

"It's a way of making a living, and we are very grateful," they would tell the onlookers. But perhaps more disturbing was the invitation to the public to prod and touch them, especially on the uncovered area of flesh that bound the two brothers together.

This was not unusual in freak shows, and it would seem the closeness of the 'audience participation' in being able to explore the exhibits with their hands as well as their eyes added to the attraction. It raises questions, however, as to exactly how freaks were viewed by the public. And perhaps just as importantly, how they were viewed by the people putting them on display. But the event at the Egyptian Hall also saw a major turning point in the development of the freak exhibition. Far from being a ramshackle travelling show it was a reputable, even scientifically educational, event in a prestigious location. With that came a level of respectability and acceptance that was to set the tone for the future.

Across the Atlantic in the USA, however, there was a rising star whose impact on the world of the freak show is arguably beyond comparison. PT Barnum was a man with huge energy and a sharp business mind. He was a firm believer in giving people what they wanted even if he had to bend the rules, and the truth, to do it. His was a world of artistic licence and, like the early pioneers of moving images that were to emerge after him, the suspension of disbelief. His enthusiastic early years in the world of the freak

Freaky Fascinations

Exhibited as the 'Missing Link', Krao had been taken from her mother under very suspicious circumstances

MY PERSONAL FASCINATION
An Interview with Dr John Woolf

What was it that inspired your interest in freak shows?
When I was around nine I watched David Lynch's film *The Elephant Man*. I was scared at the sight of the Elephant Man but felt compassion for the person behind the deformities, Joseph Merrick. That film sparked a 20-year obsession, which culminated in my book.

What was the most difficult part of your research into freak shows?
The structure! How to select and arrange the stories and the analysis in an accessible way that tells a broader history of the freak show. That was my challenge – I'll let you judge if I was successful!

In approaching the subject, what did you personally have to come to terms with?
Regrettably, due to the nature of the sources, there's a lot we don't know about freak performers, so imbuing them with agency and subjectivity was an almost impossible task. Plus, finding the right language to discuss the individuals and the subject was something I had to consider at length.

Which individual story and experience stands out for you?
Julia Pastrana, the 'Baboon Lady' who was reportedly kind and compassionate, married her showman, gave birth to a baby boy and was embalmed by her showman-cum-husband after she died. Her story brings together love, tragedy and exploitation.

What differences do you hope your work has made in the understanding of freak shows and how do you think a modern world should remember them?
I hope that people will have a clearer sense of the humanity behind the freakery: an awareness of the talented performers who transformed popular culture. I also hope people will learn that the freak show was never a marginal affair but a central part of 19th century culture, and that it's legacy still reverberates today in everything from 'fake news' to social media to our TV screens and gossip magazines.

Dr John Woolf is a writer, historian and the author of *The Wonders: Lifting The Curtain On The Freak Show, Circus And Victorian Age*

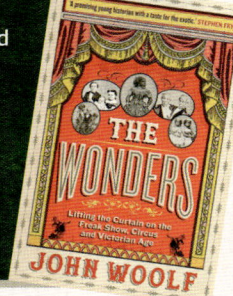

17

show were a mixture of success and disappointment, with two very public exposés of fakes in the form of the Feejee Mermaid and the supposed 161-year-old nurse of George Washington, Joice Heth, threatening to ruin his reputation.

But ever confident in his abilities to persuade and dazzle the public, Barnum was not to be deterred. As an early master of publicity and the power of advertising he forged on relentlessly to greater things. Having bought the American Museum on New York's Broadway - one of many 'Dime Museums' at the time - he set about turning it into a centre of entertainment like no other, and affordable to all. Within its walls visitors could marvel at a huge collection of wild animals and, of course, gape and wonder at the many freak performers that Barnum had begun to employ. The museum was a huge success and the showman went from strength to strength. But it was to be his discovery of a tiny boy of just four years old and a mere 25 inches high that was to propel him to international acclaim. Because of his height, Charles Stratton was already a curiosity worthy of any freak show. But as his stage persona General Tom Thumb he was to become arguably the very first international celebrity the world had ever seen.

He was an instant success, and even in a world that traded in difference he was unique. Despite his height he was not like other dwarfs, being a normally proportioned human despite his diminutive stature. And nor was he a curiosity to be merely stared

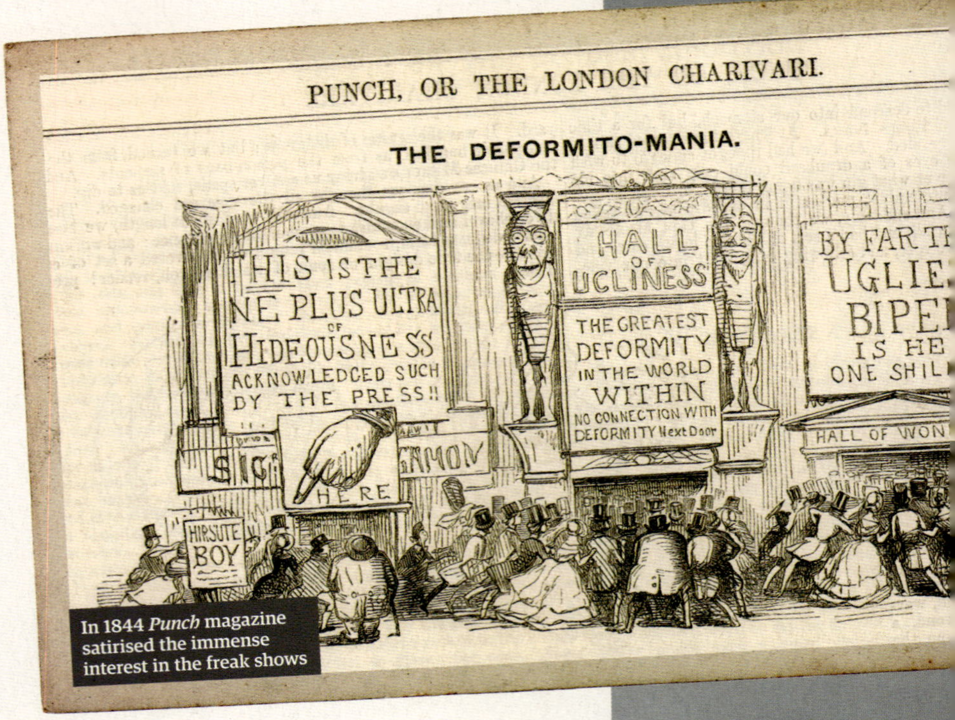

In 1844 *Punch* magazine satirised the immense interest in the freak shows

FREAKY FAKES

What you see is not always what you get

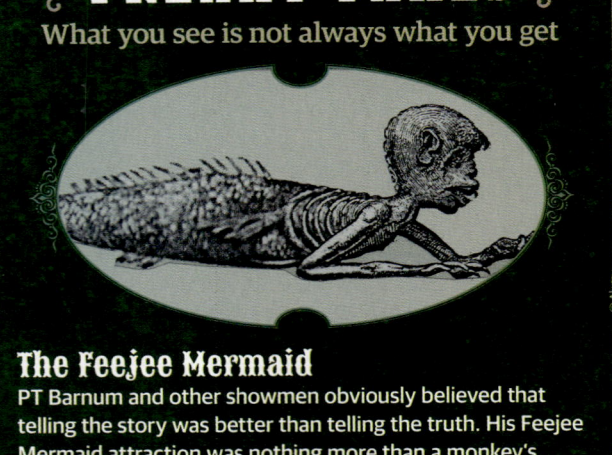

The Feejee Mermaid

PT Barnum and other showmen obviously believed that telling the story was better than telling the truth. His Feejee Mermaid attraction was nothing more than a monkey's mummified body sewn onto a large fish tail. Some may have felt cheated, but most loved the story and were excited and curious to view it anyway!

Joice Heth

Another of Barnum's tricks was to exhibit an infirm African American slave woman called Joice Heth. It was claimed she was 161 and had been the nursemaid of George Washington. Despite the fact that Heth could hardly move except lift her arm to smoke a pipe, and hardly spoke, crowds flocked to see her. When she died it was discovered she was no more than 80 and a fake. But even then Barnum made a show of it and charged people 50 cents to view the post mortem!

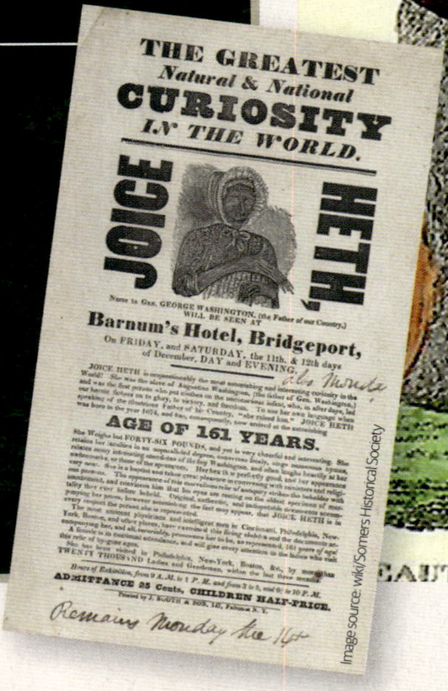

Image source: wiki/Somers Historical Society

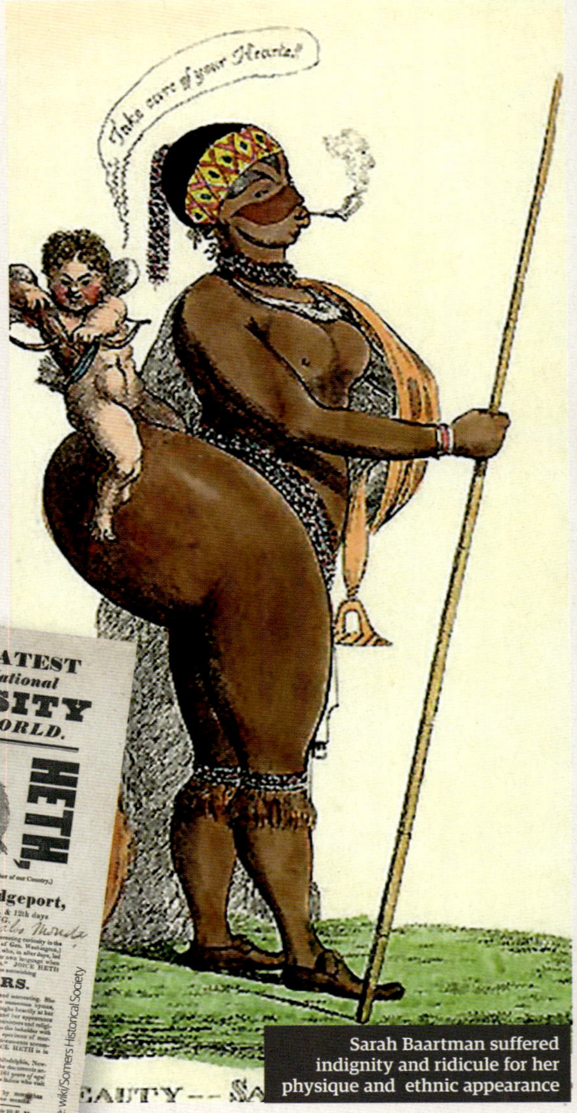

Sarah Baartman suffered indignity and ridicule for her physique and ethnic appearance

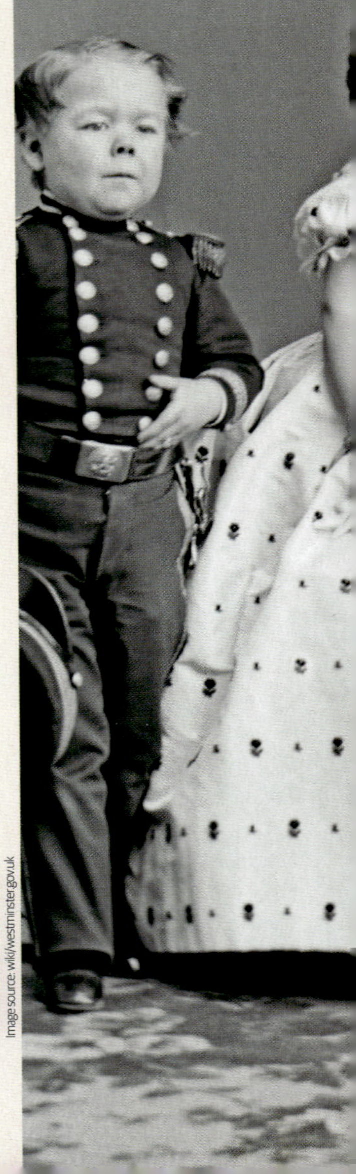

Image source: wiki/westminster.gov.uk

Freaky Fascinations

Barnum and Charles Stratton (General Tom Thumb) created the first global celebrity

at and prodded by a curious public. Here was a performer: a singer, dancer and storyteller. His audience in 1844 with Queen Victoria was a huge success. Both she and Albert were great fans of the freak show and were happy to give their support to such an entertaining and fascinating performer, sparking what *Punch* magazine called 'Deformito-Mania'. There could be no greater level of acceptance and respectability for the public at large to follow than royal approval. His tours in Britain and Europe brought him, and Barnum, fame and fortune.

But he was not alone in giving added value to the world of the freak show. The Siamese Twins had brought a physical dynamic to their performances of tumbles and acrobatics. However, middle class audiences in slightly more up-market venues with money to burn were becoming far more discerning and demanding in the sophistication of their entertainments, even from freak performers.

On first impression Julia Pastrana was the archetypal freak show exhibit. Her body and face were covered in coarse hair, her jaw protruding forwards and her lips so thick as to give the impression she had a second set of teeth. Billed as the 'Bear Woman' and sometimes 'Baboon Lady' or the 'Non-Descript', her appearance completely contradicted her personality even

> "SHE WAS AN EXHIBIT; AN EXOTIC ODDITY FROM A DISTANT MYSTERIOUS LAND TO BE STUDIED AND EXAMINED, AND CERTAINLY NOT 'ONE OF US'"

in a world full of contradictions. She was an accomplished dancer, musician and singer, with what those who met her called a ready wit and charm and the ability to speak a number of languages. In short, like Tom Thumb, Julia was a performer, not just a static curiosity. She toured and exhibited with great success throughout Europe and, despite her manager husband being an unscrupulous crook, made a very good living.

Unlike Tom Thumb, however, the curiosity surrounding Julia had a more sinister side, one of many which cast an indelible black shadow over freak shows as an industry. Sarah Baartman – The Hottentot Venus – was a South African native woman exhibited in the early years of the 19th century. Dressed in a skin-tight costume, it was the large size of her buttocks that were central to the interest of those paying to see her and she was the focus of both curiosity and ridicule. In the eyes of the audience she was an exhibit; an exotic oddity from a distant mysterious land to be studied and examined, and certainly not 'one of us'.

As European powers sailed the globe to secure territory and wealth, their exploration brought discovery of new lands and new peoples, bringing them back to fire the imaginations of a nation. It is of wonder that Victoria, as queen of the largest empire on Earth, had such an interest in what, in the freak shows industry, was known as the exotic.

There were many fairs and shows that exhibited 'exotic peoples' – from Native Americans to Inuit, Fijian and Oriental. In the same way as the 'born freaks' of conjoined twins, dwarfs, giants and limbless performers gave onlookers a growing understanding and confidence in their own physical normality, the exotic freaks were a means by which to judge how civilised and superior white Western culture was compared to such

Society & Culture

The Elephant Man Joseph Merrick was constantly studied during his life

'savages'. In the age of Darwin and the heated debate around the ancestry of mankind this played straight into the hands of the freak show owners. Julia was billed as the offspring of a union between animal and human. The young child Krao, again unnaturally covered in hair, was displayed and exhibited as the 'Missing Link', living proof that at some distant point in the past man and apes were one and the same.

And so, in a world desperate for order and structure in the way of things, Pastrana never managed to get past the point of being a freak. Despite marriage and the birth of a child (which sadly only lived for a short time), she would forever be the Baboon Lady, an animal with no soul. Following her death she was embalmed along with her dead child, dressed in her performance gown, and exhibited in London in a glass case, stripped of her dignity, a timeless exhibit for an ever-curious world.

In obtaining and exhibiting freak performers, showmen had never had too many principles or scruples, ranging from criminal to outright immoral, and lies came easily. When exhibiting Tom Thumb, Barnum claimed he was 11 when in reality he was merely four. The performer's parents were involved, but it's debatable as to whether any payment was a contract or a purchase. The young Thai child Krao was literally plucked from her home, her mother paid in cash for the inconvenience. At such a young age any consent to be exhibited from the performer herself was non-

> **"MANY SHOWMEN INVOLVED WERE GUILTY OF REGARDING THEIR PERFORMERS AS THEIR PROPERTY; OBJECTS TO BE DISPLAYED AND TRADED"**

existent. Millie and Christine, the conjoined twins known as the 'Two Headed Nightingale' were born into slavery, and stayed as such for many years even while performing their singing and dancing routine around the world, including for Queen Victoria. While their past was never actively hidden, for the freak industry to seemingly condone slavery demonstrates just how low the bar had been set in the pursuit of profit. In fact, the many showmen involved were guilty of regarding their performers as their property; objects to be displayed and traded.

For the performers themselves there was also a very human side to the story. In the freak shows they were not alone. A camaraderie grew as it does with any troupe of performers. Nor were they on the shadowy margins of society, but in the thick of it. Friendships and even relationships were not uncommon. At the wedding in London of the two giant performers Martin Bates and Anna Swan (each around eight feet) Millie and Christine were the bridesmaids. It was a widely reported and popular story, injecting a tiny bit of normality into the otherwise topsy-turvy world of the freak performers. And for those who reached the dizzy heights of national and international fame there were riches to be had, causing one freak performer to state, "If they think I'm being exploited they haven't seen my pay cheque!"

As the public appetite for entertainment grew, so did the shows. Not to be outdone, or literally miss the boat, the pioneering showmen Barnum and James Bailey created the Barnum and Bailey Circus; but with typical flair, an eye for publicity and a huge dose of arrogance it was billed as The Greatest Show On Earth! They crossed the Atlantic to England with a huge number of performers, a truly mouth-watering spectacle of

Freaky Fascinations

The Siamese twins, seen here in later years with the trappings of wealth and an air of Westernised society

Daniel Lambert's apparent love of gaming and hunting made him an archetypal image for the English gentleman

Seen with her parents, Anna Swan was about eight feet tall and her wedding to fellow giant Martin Bates made international news

vivid sounds, smells and colours. Clowns, horses, trapeze artists, exotic animals - and people - and, of course, an ever-expanding number of freaks. Except that now there was a new development to add to tantalise the senses - the Side Show. Flanking the main entrance to the Big Top, with huge colourful banners depicting the weird and wonderful exhibits, at the very tops of their voices talkers paced the platform and invited the crowds to step inside and see the wonders of the world! And now the 'born' freaks and the 'exotic' freaks were joined by the 'self-made freaks'. Sword swallowers, fire eaters, snake charmers, tattooed ladies, contortionists, strong men (and women) and performers who could pierce their bodies with swords and needles but feel no pain whatsoever.

It was an extravaganza like no other, at a price all could afford, with visitors invited to be up close with the performers, totally immersed in the outlandish experience and ready for the main event in the Big Top.

However, even now the cracks in the future of the freak show were beginning to appear. Many fairs around England were closed under vagrancy laws, cutting off the life blood of the travelling shows. In main cities equally strict councils banned public displays of freaks. One notable victim of this clampdown was Joseph Merrick, the famous Elephant Man, who was to be given refuge of sorts in the Royal London Hospital by Dr Frederick Treves. An act of kindness perhaps, although Treves' first act following Merrick's death was to dissect him and put his skeleton on display, a fate that also awaited many conjoined twins. All in the name of science, of course. And it was the rapidly growing field of medicine that was to take control of how freaks were perceived in society. By the latter part of the Victorian era the understanding of the human body, its functions and flaws, had improved immeasurably. Diseases of the flesh and of the mind now had names and therefore identities, and sufferers needed to be cared for in institutions, not put on public display. The myth and the marvel were gone, and with the early years of the 20th century came the gruesome terrors of modern warfare and its own brand of physical horror.

The public's appetite for such intrusive exhibition was fading and the world was being filled with more sophisticated, less disturbing and contentious entertainments. But like all good performers the freak shows had given their all to entertain, helping their audiences escape the drudgery of their ordinary lives and just feel good about themselves. And in that lies the real identity of the artists themselves; the inner humanity that shines through in spite of physical difference, and the empathy they had for their fellow human beings against all odds. We know the true stories and feelings of far too few of the men and women of the freak shows, and with time their tales and voices become ever fainter. It was an industry filled with sinister dark shadows, but in spite of this it was the performers themselves, their courage, their energy and their ability to face their difference with a special kind of dignity and grace that remains a lesson for us even to this day.

MEDICINE NOT MYSTERY
New understanding and new language for a new age

Proteus Syndrome
Suffered by Joseph Merrick, the famous Elephant Man. It's an overgrowth of bones, tissue, skin and organs resulting in the external growths that dominated his appearance

Microcephaly
A narrowing and reduction in the size of the skull. Sufferers were billed as 'Pin Heads' and in one famous case, simply as 'What Is It'?

Adenoma
A tumour of the pituitary gland that causes an excessive amount of growth hormone. It's more than likely the cause of most giantism of performers such as Anna Swan and her husband Martin Bates

Mental disability
Perhaps the most disturbing of all freak show conditions, where lack of mental development and learning difficulties were displayed through such acts as 'The Wild Men of Borneo'

Hyperrichosis
Bearded ladies were linked to this, but in the extreme cases it would result in performers such as Jo Jo the Dog Faced Boy.

Conjoined twins
The way their bodies were joined varied greatly. Some would share just ligaments but others would share organs and vital blood vessels, so their separation at this time would lead to certain death.

Society & Culture

A Sour Note – Vinegar Valentines

Roses are red, violets are blue, when it comes to my valentine, it sure won't be you!

Written by Bee Ginger

In the days before texts, apps and emails, letters and cards were widely exchanged, not by carrier pigeon but delivered by hand. And in the case of vinegar valentines, most likely at great speed, as these were not your average greeting card filled with soppy poetry and declarations of love. Instead they contained greetings of a much less friendly sentiment; often crass, sarcastic, cynical, emotionally damaging and downright mean-spirited. Emerging in the 1840s, the cards were originally produced in America by a number of esteemed printing companies. The trend soon spread across the pond to England, where the cards were produced not only by various stationers but publishers including none other than Raphael Tuck and Sons, the revered publishers favoured by Queen Victoria herself, to whom she granted the royal warrant of appointment.

Also known as "comic valentines" or "mocking valentines", vinegar valentines were sent anonymously, meaning the recipient would have to work out who disliked them enough to send them such a thing. A vinegar valentine could still make a person blush, only in this case with hurt, humiliation and embarrassment. Worse still, before 1840, postage was paid for by the person receiving a letter, rather than the sender. This added insult to injury, particularly if the card was aimed at someone frugal or deemed to be penny pinching.

Cheaply made and printed on a thin single sheet of paper, the majority of cards had both an insulting illustration or caricature on the front paired with an equally offensive poem. Everyone in society was targeted as an object of ridicule, from nagging wives to unfaithful lovers; even the poor old postman was not exempt from ridicule. Insults were aimed at laziness, vanity, stupidity, drunkenness and social ills, to name but a few, and as the women's suffrage movement took hold there were even cards aimed at questioning a woman's right to vote. One depicted a po-faced woman sitting in a chair clutching a book in one hand and pointing with the other, that carried the message "Your vote from me you will not get, I don't want a preaching suffragette." Men would also send the cards to their friends mocking their characteristics or chosen professions, even highlighting the reason why they were still single.

A Sour Note - Vinegar Valentines

Senders of these cards filled with insulting rhymes and garish caricatures were like the 1800s equivalent of today's internet trolls

The cards were not durable and many were destroyed by the recipients, which makes them very rare to come by. Many were also confiscated by the postal service, who would intervene and refuse to deliver the very worst cards

There was a card to target almost every insult imaginable; looks and intelligence were all targets of ridicule and so-called humour. There were even some cards that wished the recipient dead

Such was the popularity of these cutting messages that in 1847 one large retailer in New York found that the amount of traditional, loving Valentine's Day cards they sold was matched by the number of sales of their acidic counterparts.

By the late 1800s, the idea of dispatching a hurtful Valentine's card had largely faded from the public consciousness, its appeal waning in an age that has become known for tact, decorum and general public decency. Some lamented the cards' vulgarity and blamed them for the overall decline in the sending of the more traditional kinds of Valentine's cards, while others simply viewed the demise of vinegar valentines as the end of a habit in a changing society. Either way, we can all be grateful that they fizzled out before our time - even if we do chuckle at the wit the Victorians so readily deployed in the name of a deftly worded insult.

> "VINEGAR VALENTINES WERE SENT ANONYMOUSLY, MEANING THE RECIPIENT WOULD HAVE TO WORK OUT WHO DISLIKED THEM ENOUGH TO SEND ONE"

Society & Culture

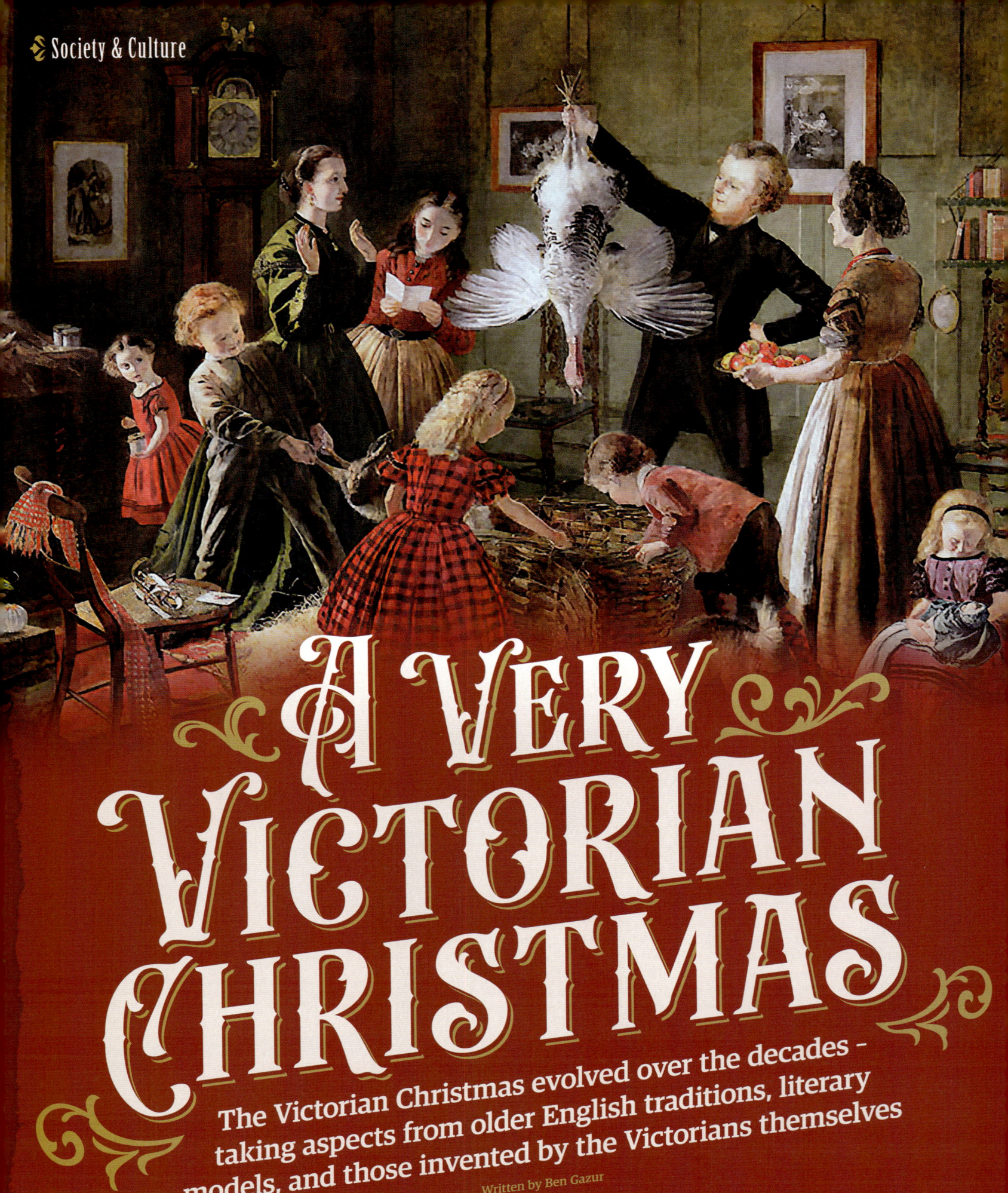

A Very Victorian Christmas

The Victorian Christmas evolved over the decades – taking aspects from older English traditions, literary models, and those invented by the Victorians themselves

Written by Ben Gazur

A Very Victorian Christmas

The celebration of Christmas in Britain was been forged across centuries by the melding of traditions from different sources. Everything from the Roman Saturnalia to the Norse pagan Yule to idiosyncratic village rituals found their way into how Christmas was observed, but by the 19th century many of these traditions were slipping away. Ever greater numbers of people were moving from the country to the city and their work in new industrial factories left them little time or opportunity for festive fun.

For all their austere tendencies the Victorians had a deeply sentimental side and were primed for a revival of Christmas. Albert, the Prince Consort, brought many Christmas traditions from his native Germany that many in the middle class wished to emulate. One of the major influences on the Victorian Christmas came from literature of the time. Charles Dickens' *A Christmas Carol* cemented the family Christmas centred on a big meal, a big turkey, and a big pudding as the ideal of Christmas everyone should strive to achieve.

While much of what we think of as a traditional Christmas is now modelled on the Victorian ideal there were many stranger aspects of their Yuletide celebrations which we no longer follow, in some cases for good reason.

The pudding became the centrepiece of the Victorian Christmas meal

PUDDING FOR EVERYONE

When should you start making your Christmas Pudding? Luckily for the Victorians there was an easy way to remember. Each year on the Sunday before Advent the vicar would read a prayer which began "Stir up, we beseech thee, O Lord..."

Though the prayer refers to spiritual matters people used the opening words as a reminder to get their pudding ready. Stir-up Sunday became a Victorian tradition. On that day everyone in the household from the master and mistress, to the children, and all the staff would take a turn stirring the mixture of the pudding for good luck.

As well as the usual dried fruit and other tasty bits of a Christmas Pudding the mixture might have had various silver charms added to it. These were used to tell people's fortune for the next year. If you got a sixpence you would be wealthy, a wishbone meant luck, and a boot represented travel.

Mistletoe gave an outlet for the repressed Victorians to share kisses.

UNDER THE MISTLETOE

Alongside bringing trees into the home Victorians also decorated with various other bits of greenery. Mistletoe has a long history in folklore and even the staid Victorians could not resist kissing under it. If a young lady refused to kiss under it then she was said to be doomed to another year of being unmarried. So popular was mistletoe that one journalist decried "the wholesale slaughter of the innocent mistletoe" for Christmas.

Snap-dragon originated in the Elizabethan period but was beloved of Victorian children

FIERY FUN AND GAMES

Entertaining children at Christmas can be tricky, but the Victorians loved a parlour game with enough danger to entice any child. Snap-dragon, sometimes called Flap-dragon, was a simple test of skill and bravery. A shallow bowl of raisins was put on the table between the players and warm brandy poured over them. This was then set ablaze and the game was to snatch up as many flaming raisins as you could and eat them. Players placed the burning fruit in their mouth and snapped it shut to extinguish the flames - hence the name of the game. Please don't try this at home.

Society & Culture

GOING A-GOODING

On St Thomas' Day, the 21st of December, in rural communities the poor members of society would go from door to door to beg for small amounts of food. This was known as Mumping, Thomasing, or Gooding and was particularly associated with old ladies. By collecting a little from each home the women were able to provide for themselves over the Christmas period. In return for the food they often handed out sprigs of mistletoe.

Acts of charity were part of Christmas for the Victorians

Christmas crackers are one tradition we can trace back to its invention

IT'S A CRACKER!

Pulling paper crackers and hearing a loud gunpowder snap is a beloved part of British Christmas dinners. They were invented by Tom Smith in 1847 as simple sugared almonds in a paper twist, but these developed into paper tubes containing a small novelty, a short poem, and the snapping explosive. He named them Cossacks, but soon everyone was calling them crackers. When Smith's son took over the company he added the paper crowns we still wear today.

Bizarre cards were common features of a Victorian Christmas

WEIRD AND WONDROUS CARDS

Christmas cards developed soon after the introduction of the Victorian penny post in 1840, but had themes you're unlikely to see today. Some show animals in unusual states - like a line of frogs with umbrellas - or macabre situations - dead robins occur more than once. Hunting a robin was once considered lucky so perhaps they were intended to foretell good fortune. Other cards show terrifying characters made of Christmas pudding or suave looking vegetable people, showing a Victorian taste for whimsy. When Father Christmas appeared on cards he was as likely to be tossing a naughty child into his sack as delivering gifts.

A Very Victorian Christmas

TURKEYS FOR CHRISTMAS

Each year around 10 million turkeys are eaten in the UK each year at Christmas, but this was not always the case. For most people goose was the traditional meat served at the festive table, and only wealthy people could afford a turkey. This is why Scrooge's gift of a huge turkey to the Cratchits in *A Christmas Carol* is so generous. Turkey became the aspirational meat for families with pretensions of class.

Turkeys, unless won in raffles, were too expensive for most families

Even if you couldn't afford a real boar's head, you could serve a cake version at Christmas

BOAR'S HEAD FEAST

Turkey may have been rich man's meat, but only the true elite could afford a boar's head feast. Scholars of Queen's College, Oxford still have a boar's head at Christmas. By the Victorian era this was already becoming outdated, but those who wanted a cheaper version found ways to make it. Cakes were shaped and decorated to mimic a wild boar's decapitated head for the Christmas table, sometimes even with bright red bloody icing.

TREES ON FIRE

Decorating evergreen trees for Christmas was a German tradition, and George III's German Queen Charlotte had one at Windsor Castle in 1800. Prince Albert created a demand for Christmas trees in Britain when he had his family drawn around their tree. This illustration of a royal Christmas was widely published and emulated in homes across the country. As well as the glass decorations we know today the Victorians hung paper chains in their trees and tied small candles onto the branches and lit them for illumination – probably too risky to try this today.

Victoria and Albert led the fashion for Christmas trees in England

HUNTING THE WREN

What to do on Boxing Day is a question that troubles many families. On the Isle of Man the boys were sent out to 'Hunt the Wren'. When they trapped and killed a wren they tied the poor bird to the top of a decorated pole and paraded it through the streets. Many of the boys would be wearing strange masks as they danced around the wren. Even some Victorian commentators thought this tradition "barbarous".

Wren Boys getting ready to parade their captured birds

Society & Culture

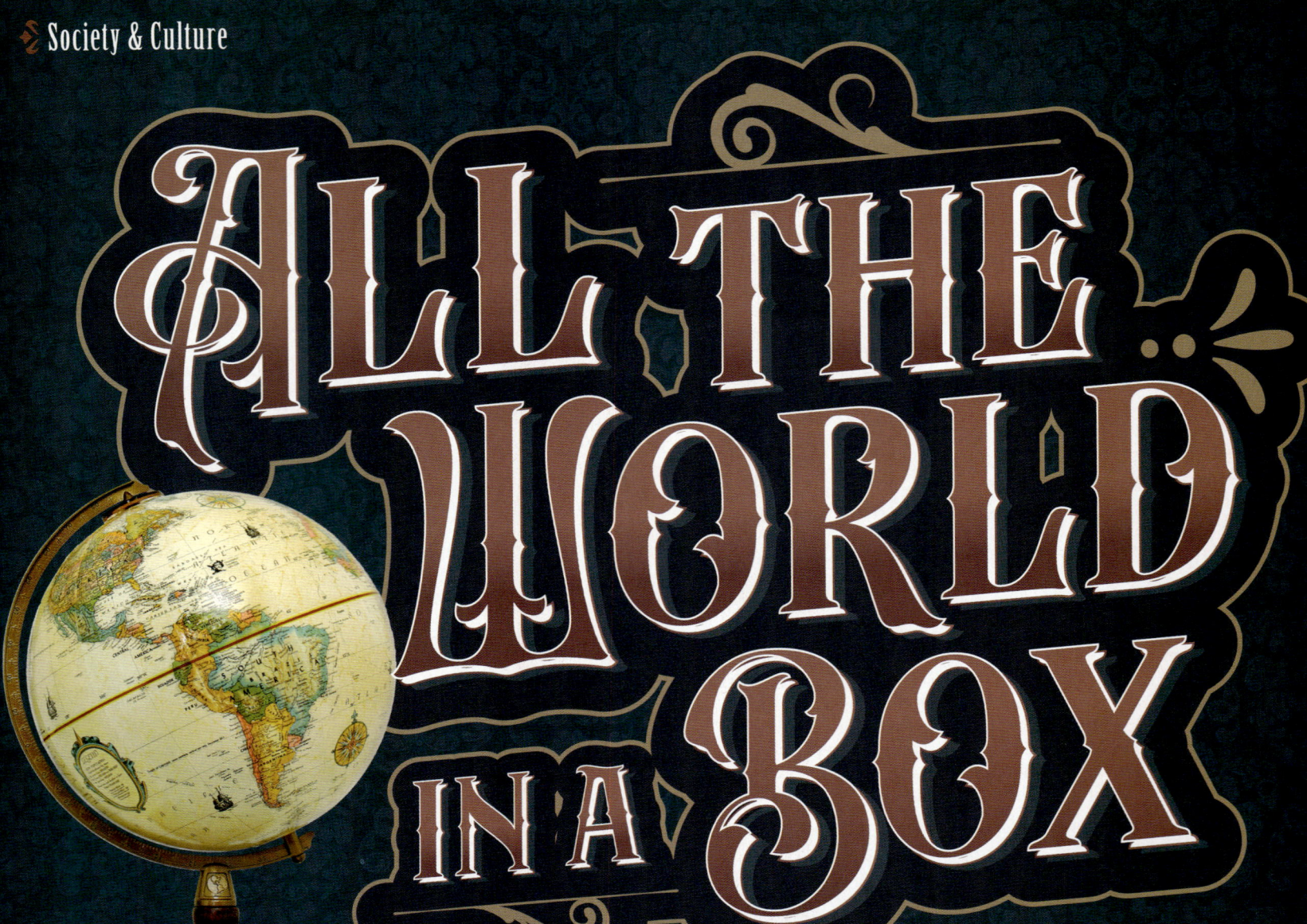

All the World in a Box

Victorian cabinets of curiosities were marvellous collections of the odd, the unusual and the bizarre

Written by Edoardo Albert

Charles Dickens wrote *The Old Curiosity Shop* between 1840 and 1841 (it was originally written in weekly instalments). The title tells the tale: that there should be a shop – an old one at that – selling 'curiosities' told of the Victorian fascination with items that they could put on display, in cabinets of curiosities. The 19th century was the peak of the curiosity cabinet. This was the era when what had previously been the preserve of kings and the nobility spread downwards through society, so that even an average middle-class family might put their collected curiosities on display.

The first 'cabinets of curiosities' were more often whole rooms displaying paintings and artworks, strange and unusual items from home and abroad, and, finally, bits of animals: narwhal tusks labelled as the horns of unicorns were popular, but so were skulls, claws, shells and feathers: anything bright, intricate or unusual. Some of these collections became the star exhibits of later museums; Sir Hans Sloane's natural history collection became the basis of the British Museum.

The cabinet that displayed these Victorian curiosities was usually made from beautifully carved hardwood, such as mahogany, with glass-panelled doors that, when closed, prevented the collection from being covered in dust – since many curiosities were delicate, it was difficult to clean them. The rear panel of the cabinet was mirrored: this made it easier to see the items at the back of the cabinet, as well as reflecting light over the collection (through most of the Victorian era, candles, lanterns and gas lights were the only source of interior light when the sun had set).

As for what the cabinet contained, collections reflected the tastes of the collector. Amateur antiquarians travelled the country, making the first archaeological excavations, and many of these finds were put on display in curio cabinets. But just as the past was opening up, so was the wider world: the British Empire was reaching its apogee, and strange and wonderful items from around the world were arriving in Britain's ports. Many Victorians also travelled abroad, collecting the wonders of the world

All the World in a Box

This early Kunstkammer (many of the first collections were in Germany) shows the eclectic mixture of curiosities, natural and man-made, that went into a typical cabinet of curiosities

To better show the objects on display, Victorian cabinets of curiosities generally had mirrored rear panels

Narwhal tusks, traded south from the indigenous people who found them, were often put on display in cabinets of curiosities as unicorn horns

and bringing them home again: butterflies, masks, human oddities (there was a brisk trade in heads supposedly shrunken by head-hunting tribes), beetles and just about everything else.

The Victorians were enthusiastic collectors of the delightfully weird and wonderful.

The cabinet of curiosities, each with its associated story, was a valuable source of entertainment both for its owner and for guests who, when visiting, would be told the stories of the wonders on display; it made a great alternative to someone playing the piano badly.

> "THE BRITISH EMPIRE WAS REACHING ITS APOGEE, AND STRANGE AND WONDERFUL ITEMS FROM AROUND THE WORLD WERE ARRIVING IN BRITAIN'S PORTS"

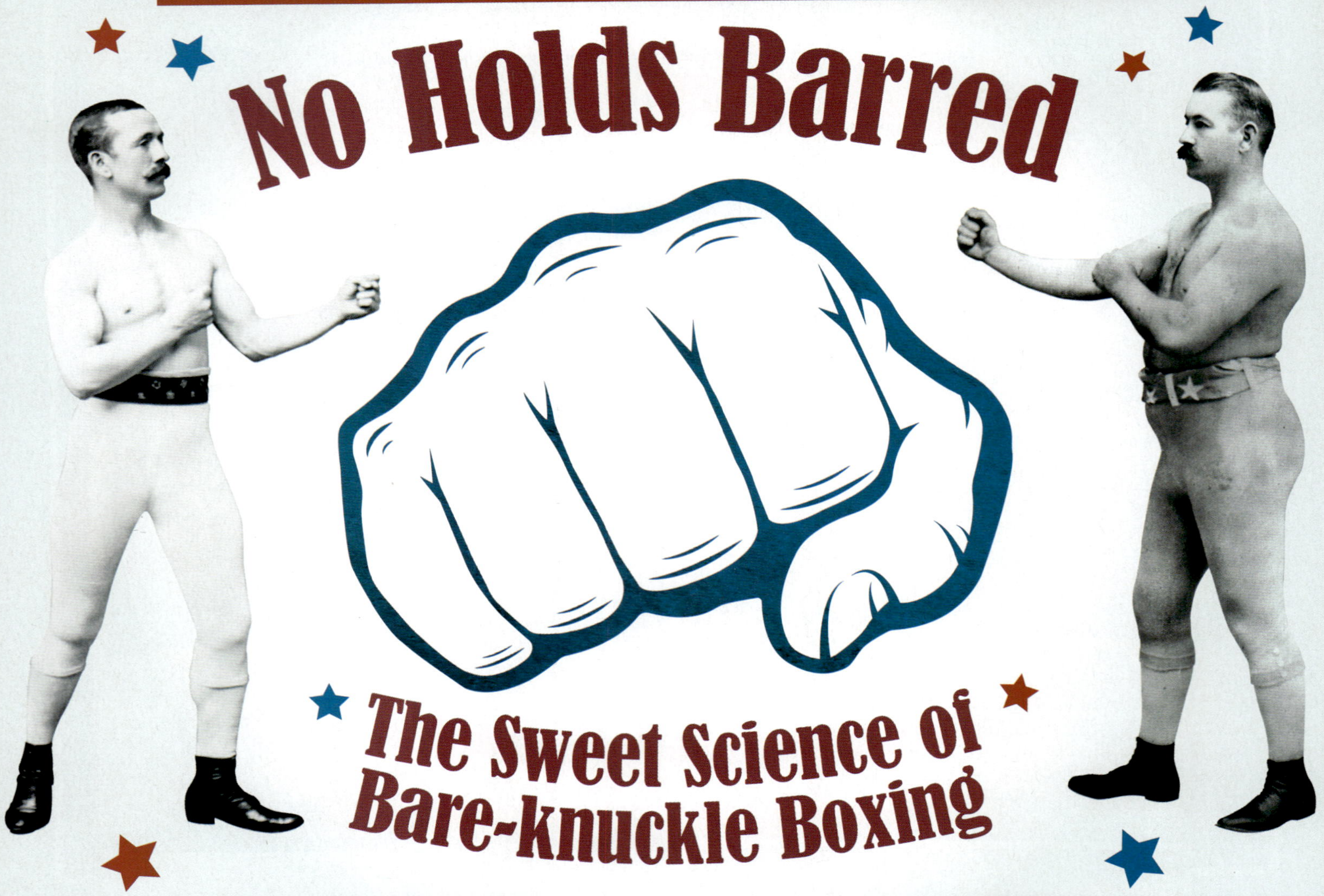

Society & Culture

No Holds Barred
The Sweet Science of Bare-knuckle Boxing

The blood-splattered truth behind Britain's underground fight club that attracted crowds of thousands – including kings and prime ministers – even after it was outlawed

Written by Paul Edwards and Robert Lock

On the morning of 17 April 1860, boxing's first-ever 'world title' match took place in a field near the small town of Farnborough, Hampshire. Billed as the 'fight of the century', the bout was between all-American champ John Heenan and England's reigning champion Tom Sayers.

The greatest of his generation, at 1.7 metres (5 foot 8 inches) tall and weighing 67 kilograms (147 pounds), Sayers had managed to punch his way up into the heavyweight division. Here he demolished his lumbering opponents through a combination of incredible skill and tenacity. However, that was in the 1850s, and 'Brighton Titch,' as Sayers was nicknamed, was now 33 – old even by modern boxing standards. In contrast, Heenan was in his mid-twenties and at the height of his powers.

He was about 1.9 metres (6 feet, 2 inches) and 43 kilograms (195 pounds), with an apparently lethal left hook. Known as the 'Benicia Boy,' Heenan grew up in New York State, but learned to fight in California, where he worked as an 'enforcer' for a San Francisco gang, before taking up the sport. Still, Heenan's training had been sporadic – unlike Sayers – and he didn't have the old pro's experience to fall back on.

The title fight gripped the imagination on both sides of the Atlantic. As *Harper's Weekly* put it: "The bulk of the people in England and America are heart and soul engrossed in a fight compared to which a Spanish bull-bait is but a mild and diverting pastime." Meanwhile, in Britain, the *Manchester Guardian* observed that "no pugilistic contest ever decided has excited so great an interest, both in this and other countries."

When the two men were called to the 'scratch' at 7.29am, you couldn't see the green grass of the field for the packed crowd that filled it. The two fighters stood in the middle of a small, roped-off area, stripped down to their waists, but they didn't don gloves – this was a bare-knuckle battle.

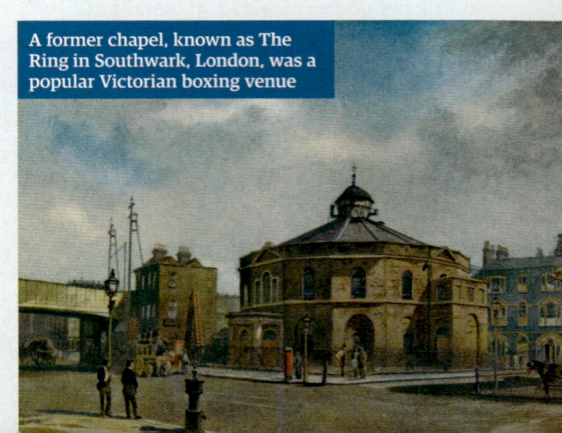
A former chapel, known as The Ring in Southwark, London, was a popular Victorian boxing venue

Newspaper sketch of Tom Sayers in his heyday, fighting Tom Paddock in 1858

First rules of Fight Club

Jack Broughton's dos and don'ts guided bareknuckle boxing for over a century

✓ Do

Come to scratch
Each boxer had to come to the centre of the ring for the fight to legally continue. If a boxer could not make the scratch under his own efforts, it was quite acceptable for his seconds to drag him there for him to be able to carry on.

The battle begins
No one could be in the ring except the fighter's seconds and the referee. Usually each fighter would have two seconds who stayed in the ring with him at all times, so at each bout there would be, including the fighters, eight or nine people.

It's a knockout
There were disputes as to how long a man should stay on the floor to declare his opponent the winner. From the knockdown, his 'seconds' had 30 seconds to again drag him to his corner and prepare him for the next round.

In the by-battles
The winning fighter should be given two thirds of the money, which would be publicly divided up on stage. This arrangement was acceptable to all parties, but some had side bets that were paid out privately after the fight.

Get it right
Show some humility and understanding in the way in which a boxer wins or loses a fight. It's not always enough to turn a back on an opponent, and in exceptional circumstances the winner may wish to donate some of his purse to the loser.

✗ Don't

Keep it clean
Once a man is down, it will not be lawful for one man to strike the other. Gouging will not be acceptable, but to grab a fighter by the throat or throw him to the ground is within the rules, though once he is there kicking is prohibited.

Use your feet
Under the Broughton Rules, feet were now strictly for standing on and not used to further injure an opponent, whether he was upright or knocked down. There will be no heavy or spiked objects within the shoe to cause unnecessary harm to the opponent.

Use your head
Head-butting prior to 1743 was an accepted practice, but times were changing, and this manoeuvre was becoming more and more unpopular. Spectators were looking for skill with the fists, not the head. The fight game was progressing in the right direction.

Holding the ropes
Holding the ropes was used to get more momentum from the body when assaulting the opponent. This, coupled with the use of resin on the hands to ensure better grip, was also outlawed and frowned upon from spectators.

Do not bite
Biting was commonplace during fights, and could inflict serious clinical issues to the recipient. This was quite rightly outlawed, as was the use of holding stones in the fists to produce more power in the punch. The fists at the end of a fight would be broken and difficult to open.

> **"Various stories claim Parliament shortened its hours so Lord Palmerston could attend"**

Both gladiators tore strips out of each other early on: Sayers was forced to fight one-handed when he injured his right arm, while Heenan was half blinded due to a swollen eye. Nonetheless, the pair duked it out for a staggering 42 rounds. Each severely bloodied and battered, they fought tit for tat for two hours and 27 minutes. However, before either champion could land a winning blow, the police arrived, wielding their truncheons, to stop the fight.

Bare-knuckle boxing was illegal, as it had been since it gained popularity in the early 18th century. However, the fights were regulated by the semi-respectable British Pugilists' Protective Association, reported on in the sport section of newspapers, and drew large crowds, including the great and good. The Heenan vs Sayers clash has been heavily mythologised: various stories claim Parliament shortened its hours so Prime Minister Lord Palmerston could attend, that novelists Charles Dickens and William Thackeray were both forced to flee the police along with the rest of the audience, while Queen Victoria sat in her palace waiting for news of the result. So how did bare-knuckle boxing come to gain such an allure in the British imagination, and why then did it disappear?

Birth of Boxiana
The first recorded prize fight in Britain took place in January 1681, with regular matches being staged at the Royal Theatre in London by 1698. However, it is perhaps too generous to call these clashes 'sport'. While we might consider the Sayers and Heenan bout ultra-violent by modern standards, they at least followed set rules. During and leading up to the 18th century, the only aim was that you had to defeat your opponent – by any means necessary. Wrestling was allowed, so a man could grab and throw his opponent, then jump on and beat him while he was down. Fists were the primary weapon, but fighters would also wield swords, cudgels or quarterstaffs. Outside of the more sophisticated theatres, they would often face each other in an ill-defined ring formed by the crowd, which would be constantly moving as eager fans pressed in or stepped back to avoid being hit. The pair would beat each other to the point where either of them could no longer carry on. The only aspects that we would really recognise – beyond the fighters – was that there was an umpire to adjudicate on who won if both contenders were badly beaten, and that each man had a second, what we would call a cornerman today, who could throw in the towel for their fighter to rescue them while forfeiting the match to the other man.

James Figg was England's greatest champion in this era. Born in Oxfordshire around 1695, probably to a poor farming family, Figg is said to only have lost one fight in a career that encompassed over 270 fights. Figg claimed he only lost because he was ill, and indeed he defeated the victor, Ned Sutton, in a rematch. Figg was even considered famous enough to be painted by William Hogarth on trading cards.

However, Figg got ahead in this anything-goes age because he was technically skilled. The Marquis de Bretagne noted that Figg, "handles a broad sword [sic] with the greatest dexterity of any man alive." By 1714, Figg had moved to London to study with the Company of Masters of the Science of Defence, a guild dating back to Tudor times that trained members to fight proficiently with rapier, quarterstaff and, of course, broadsword. Figg qualified as a 'master' in under a year. While training, Figg also fought at a fair in Southwark. He would lure crowds to his booth by declaring: "Here I am, Jemmy Figg from Thame – I will fight any man in England!"

In 1719, Figg opened an 'academy of arms' just off Oxford Street. Here, he taught pupils – from aspiring

31

Society & Culture

professional prize fighters to gentlemen about town – new techniques, adapting what he knew from the art of swordplay for boxing, including how to block and cross-punch.

While Figg raised the quality of the sport, it was one of his students, Jack Broughton, who laid down the rules. Like Figg, he fought at a fairground, but was profoundly affected when he accidentally killed his opponent, George Stephenson, in 1741. When Stephenson – who was another student of Figg's – fell and didn't get up, Broughton is said to have cried, "Good God. What have I done? I've killed him. So help me God, I'll never fight again."

He didn't keep to this oath, but two years later he opened Broughton's Amphitheatre and changed boxing forever. The new proprietor outlined seven rules, which he taught to his students and insisted upon being followed in every fight. These still allowed wrestling moves and even hair-pulling, but the weapons were removed and contenders were forbidden to hit a man when he was down or when he was on his knees. Broughton also insisted that a "square of a yard" be chalked in the middle of the stage; when a man was knocked down, he would have half a minute to return to the mark with the help of his second, or be declared defeated. While he only intended to govern bouts taking place in his own ring, the Broughton Rules, as they became known, were quickly adopted by other venues and continued to guide the sport for the next 100 years.

Regency Royal Rumble

In 1750, an Act of Parliament reaffirmed that prize fighting was illegal. The courts would charge contenders with affray or assault, while spectators ran the risk of being classified as disorderly assemblies. The law continued to be widely flouted, but its reiteration may have had something to do with the temporary decline in interest among the gentry. The sport was also beset by corruption at this time, with fight after fight being thrown. Jack Slack, a savage fighter and grandson of James Figg, is credited with being the first known person to fix a fight. He is believed to have paid off better fighters to lose in other matches to stop top contenders challenging his title. After losing it anyway to William

> **" The Broughton Rules, as they became known, were quickly adoped by venues "**

Daniel Mendoza holds his opponent in a headlock

No Holds Barred

Two men spar on a wintery 26th December - but 'Boxing day' wasn't named for the sport

Ben Caunt raises Ben Bendigo up by the neck in an 1845 showdown

Stevens in 1760, Slacks then paid Stevens to take a fall against his protege, George Meggs.

This downturn continued for 30 years until someone came along who could bet on a fight without fear of the law or loss of earnings: the Prince of Wales. The future George IV attended a number of bare-knuckle-boxing matches between 1786 and 1788. Most notably, he watched 'Gentleman' John Jackson's victory over William Futrell on 9 July 1788. With such a prominent figure holding court ringside, 'the Fancy' – as prize fighters called the upper classes – soon came flocking back.

Based on his nickname, it's perhaps unsurprising that the aforementioned 'Gentleman' Jackson helped legitimise the sport. Originally from a fairly well-to-do family, Jackson ran a boxing academy for gentry, most notably including the poet Lord Byron among his students. For George IV's coronation, Jackson was asked to assemble guards to keep order, and chose 18 prize fighters.

However, while these fighters won over the nobility, in London's East End, a Jewish fighter of Portuguese descent named Daniel Mendoza pioneered a crucial new technique. Up until this time, boxers had relied on stinging like a bee, not floating like a butterfly. Only 1.7 metres (5 feet 7 inches) tall and weighing 72.5 kilograms (160 pounds), the slight fighter was the first to emphasise rapid, rather than hard, punching, as well as thinking seriously about his footwork so that he could win through speed rather than brute strength.

With the sport at all-time high, in 1812, journalist Pierce Egan went as far to claim boxing defined British identity. In his book *Boxiana*, Egan wrote that without it the national character might "act too refined and the thorough-bred bulldog degenerate into the whining puppy! Not for the British the long knives of the Dutch, Italian stilettos or French or German sticks and stones – in England the fist only is used [...] As a national trait we feel no hesitation in declaring that it is wholly British!" We can perhaps

Top 5 Prize Fighters
These boxers, without doubt, were the real superstars of their day

Tom Cribb
8 July 1781 – 11 May 1848

Born in Bristol to a coal worker father, Tom Cribbs began his career in 1805. It may be debatable whether he would have gained as much prominence if it were not for his two fights against the 'Black American', Tom Molineaux. His defining bout was the Molineaux rematch of 1811 in front of 20,000 fight fans, such was the popularity of the sport. He's still much loved in his home city of Bristol.

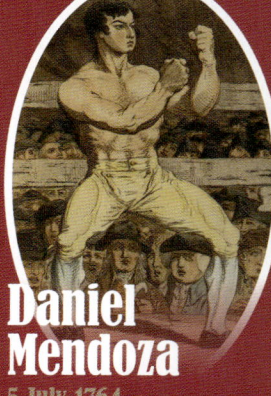

Daniel Mendoza
5 July 1764 – 3 September 1836

Dan was the first Jewish champion of England, and possibly the world, depending on how we interpret his fights. He took boxing to another level with his skill, style and speed. He abandoned the wrestling moves and worked on the scientific approach to all his fights. Not the biggest of fighters, he readily took on - and beat - opponents several stone heavier than himself.

Tom Molineaux
1784 – 4 August, 1818

Molineaux's exact date of birth is unknown, because he was born a slave on a Virginia plantation. However, he became known for fighting other slaves there, and after victory upon victory he was granted his greedom. Two very notable fights against Tom Cribb in 1810 and 1811 at Thistleton Gap in the East Midlands saw 20,000 people witness his defeat of Tom Cribb. He died in Galway in 1818.

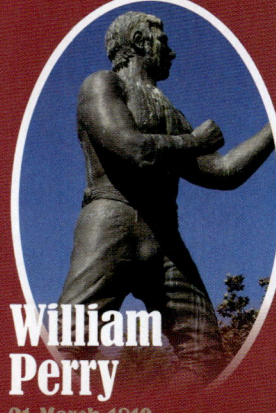

William Perry
21 March 1819 – 18 January 1881

Known as the 'Tipton Slasher', he became Heavyweight Champion of England in 1850 after beating Tom Paddock. Soon after this, he suffered a controversial defeat to Henry Broome on a referee's decision. Later he regained the coveted title, before eventually losing it to Tom Sayers in 1857. He was born with a severe deformity in his left leg that impacted his walk, which led some people to refer to him as 'K Legs'.

John Gully
21 August 1783 – 9 March 1863

Another Bristolian, in his early years he was imprisoned in a debtor's institution, but later became a prize fighter. The Duke of Clarence (later King William IV) witnessed his brutal 64-round fight against Henry Pearce in 1805. In the latter half of his life, he was an entrepreneur and race horse owner. He also became a politician, and sat in the House of Commons as the MP for Pontefract from 1832 to 1837.

Birth of Women's Boxing

Very little is known about women's boxing during the 19th century, perhaps because it was seen as a sideshow and not reflective of the way men went about their fights. Some of these tough women fought bare chested and, by some illogical reasoning, wore long dresses down to the floor to hide their modesty. Many prostitutes also took part in the matches. Usually the women would fight with a coin in each hand, and the first to drop it would be deemed the loser.

The first recorded fight between two females took place in 1722 near what is now, Oxford Circus between Elizabeth Wilkinson and Martha Jones. Wilkinson won the contest and was considered to be the first female champion, and she fought fully clothed, so the audience would take her more seriously. Wilkinson would have been born around 1700, but the details of her birth cannot be proved with any certainty. However, it seems she became a very formidable fighter not only with her fists, but also with a dagger, cudgel and quarterstaff. Elizabeth went on to marry a pugilist named Stokes, who fought in James Figg's boxing booth and eventually set up her own booth to rival Figg's.

In 1722 she handed out a challenge to Hannah Hyfield of Newgate Market. It was usual for women's fights to last between 20 minutes and an hour, and Elizabeth's strength and fitness far exceeded the low expectations of female stamina at the time. Elizabeth Wilkinson Stokes, as she became known, had a close rival in Mary Welsh (who, ironically, was Irish).

The two women fought, along with their husbands, forming 'mixed-doubled' pairs. From all accounts it seems Welsh won the battle, although this cannot be proven with any certainty.

chalk some of this nationalism up to the fact that Egan was writing during the Napoleonic War, but boxing's hold upon the British imagination is evidenced in the many idioms taken from the sport that entered the English language during this period. Phrases such as 'start from scratch' (to start over from the beginning), and 'not up to the mark' (not up to the necessary level) may refer to the line that was scratched in the dirt to divide the ring. It's said the term 'draw', meaning a tied score, derives from the stakes that held the rope surrounding the ring; when the match was over, the stakes were 'drawn' out from the ground. These stakes might also be the basis behind the monetary meaning of stakes. In early prize fights, a bag of money, which would go to the winner of the bout, was hung from one of the stakes – thus high stakes and stake money.

The Regency era (1811-20) proved to be a golden age for bare-knuckle boxing, producing a constellation of superstars, including Tom Belcher, Tom Cribb, John Gully, and Bill Richmond – another former slave who spent most of his career in Britain. However, it was the year of Queen Victoria's coronation, 1838, that saw bare-knuckle boxing take a step forward. The London Prize Ring rules – also called the London Rules for brevity – were quickly adopted on both sides of the Atlantic, introducing a larger 7.3-metre (24-foot) ring enclosed by rope, declaring that fallen fighters should be able to return to the mark unaided or forfeit the match, and forbid butting, gouging, hitting below the waist and kicking as fouls.

KO in the UK

After the police interrupted Sayers and Heenan's fight for the world title in 1860, there was a dispute over who actually won. Officially, the referee declared it a draw, but Heenan demanded a rematch. This never happened, instead the pair both received a championship belt and split the 'purse' of £400 – over £20,000 in today's money. When Heenan

Bare-knuckle boxing was a fixture of British sport for 200 years

returned to the United States he was given a hero's welcome anyway and 50,000 New Yorkers came out to welcome him.

Meanwhile, Sayers fans raised £3,000 so that the veteran fighter could retire. However, the next five years didn't go well for him. Sayers divorced and had several other acrimonious break-ups, suffered from diabetes and tuberculosis, made a failed investment in a circus, and developed a drinking problem. He died living above a shop on Camden High Street at the age of 39. What was left of Sayers' still sizeable

The illegal sport attracted high society fans in the 18th Century

No Holds Barred

Padded gloves were introduced as a safety measure under the 1867 Queensberry Rules

Jake Kilrain takes on John Sullivan in 1889, the last recognised bareknuckle fight

fortune was spent on an extravagant funeral. Some 100,000 people took part in his procession as Sayer's loyal mastiff dog, Lion, wearing a crepe ruff, led his coffin to Highgate Cemetery.

In some ways, the fates of the two men signalled the shift in bare-knuckle boxing's fortunes in the two countries. Corruption once again emerged in the British sport, with more fights being rigged. Meanwhile, Victorian moralists decried bare-knuckle boxing for its violence. Seizing on growing popular opinion, Parliament increasingly penalised the game in such a way that every fight fan or fighter would be arrested and dealt with accordingly if caught in the act of promoting or supporting a prize fight.

After Sayer, Britain still produced a few acclaimed bruisers, most notably Tom King and Jem Mace. Facing growing persecution at home and the promise of greater cash prizes abroad, these fighters increasingly went to the US. The sport was illegal there too, but the law varied state by state, and in some places it was quite lax. Mace courted the fame the sport brought in the US, where he continued to fight until he was well into his 60s.

In 1882, rising Boston talent John L Sullivan beat Irish-born Paddy Ryan in a highly publicised bout in Mississippi City. *The New York Times* claimed some $300,000 was wagered across America on the fight, while telegraph circuits surged to deliver blow-by-blow accounts to eager fans that filled the streets. At last, it seemed America had embraced prize fighting and the spiritual home of the sport had finally moved across the Atlantic. However, at this point the sport's days were numbered all around the world.

> **The fates of two men signalled the shift in bare-knuckle boxing's fortunes**

In 1867, the Marquess of Queensberry endorsed a new set of rules for boxing. Though actually written by a Welsh sportsman named John Graham Chambers, the most important detail of the Queensberry Rules was the biggest change to the sport since Jack Broughton laid down the law in 1743. It demanded that all fighters wear padded boxing gloves.

While bare-knuckle fighting didn't end overnight, Jem Mace was quick to see that the writing was on the wall. Changing his tactics, the former English heavyweight champion defeated the formidable Bill Davis in Virginia City, Nevada, under the Queensberry Rules in 1876. The last bare-knuckle fight took place on British soil in 1885 between champion Jem Smith and Jack Davis. Smith won easily, but few witnessed the spectacle.

The Queensberry code came into force in the United States and Canada in the late 19th century, with the last recognised bare-knuckle encounter taking place on 8 July 1889, between Jake Kilrain and John L Sullivan. Fought using the London Rules, this contest ran until an incredible 76 rounds, when Kilrain's second threw in the sponge, saying his man would die if the bout went on any longer. With that, bare-knuckle boxing was served its final KO.

Or was it? That was the case until this June, when the first legal bare-knuckle boxing match was held in the US – almost 130 years since the last match. Arnold Adams and DJ Lindermann met for their showdown in the prairie city of Cheyenne, Wyoming. 2,000 fans crammed into the converted ice rink, and after a gruelling set, Arnold Adams won. Other states are now looking to legalise the fights.

With bare-knuckle boxing poised to get back in the ring once again, it's all the more important to recall the working-class origins of the bloody sport.

The East End slums where many British bare-knuckle fighters grew up

35

Society & Culture

BABY FARMING

If a family could not support a new arrival, they could be tragically sold to so-called 'baby farmers' to help make ends meet

Written by Jack Griffiths

If a child was born to a family that couldn't support them, there was no social security in Victorian Britain to help. Parents in poverty, who couldn't look after a child for fear of missing out on a workhouse wage, were left with an awful option, baby farming. The social pressure of having a child out of wedlock often forced this decision. The Poor Law of 1834 helped support working families in workhouses but gave little or no help to single mothers. The policy's Bastardy Clause even meant the father of an illegitimate child was not responsible for their welfare.

Baby farming was the selling of children by people who couldn't or wouldn't look after them. The babies could go directly to richer, childless couples for often only a few pounds, but some infants would be sold to the baby farmers - groups who found babies new homes and families for cash. Some baby farmers were genuinely helping unwanted children and desperate families. However, many nefarious groups and individuals were only in it for the money. In tragic circumstances, if some baby farmers couldn't find a suitable buyer, or became overwhelmed with too many babies, they would leave children to die, safe in the knowledge that they have already received their profit from the family that was unable to care for the infant. Even more well-meaning adopters, could become unable to feed, shelter and clothe children, after the initial money from the baby farming ran out.

Adverts would be placed in newspapers asking if anyone could adopt the baby, or baby famers would place their own ads. One such advert was submitted by someone called Amelia Dyer, promising a safe and loving home. As it turned out, Dyer would become a serial killer who is believed to have murdered as many as 400 children over 30 years for financial gain. With little record kept of these transactions, and many children dying young at this time, Dyer got away with her despicable scheme for almost two decades until she was hanged for her crimes after a body was found in the River Thames, and detectives traced it back to her. In the wake of the trial, adoption laws were made stricter to help prevent more abhorrent examples like the one of Dyer. More powers were provided to investigate baby farmers in the late 19th and early 20th centuries and the practice, thankfully, dissolved.

Baby Farming

Families were simply unable to look after the child and left with no other option, with baby farmers keen to make some easy money

With very little contraception and abortion illegal, many illegitimate children were born straight into poverty in the Victorian era

Amelia Dyer, the notorious Ogress of Reading, was a serial killer who murdered the infants in her care for money

> "SOME BABY FARMERS WERE GENUINELY HELPING DESPERATE FAMILIES. HOWEVER, MANY WERE ONLY IN IT FOR THE MONEY"

Society & Culture

SUN, SEA AND SOCIAL BREAKDOWN

The rise of the railway brought seaside resorts in reach of the masses — and fresh challenges to maintain Victorian morality

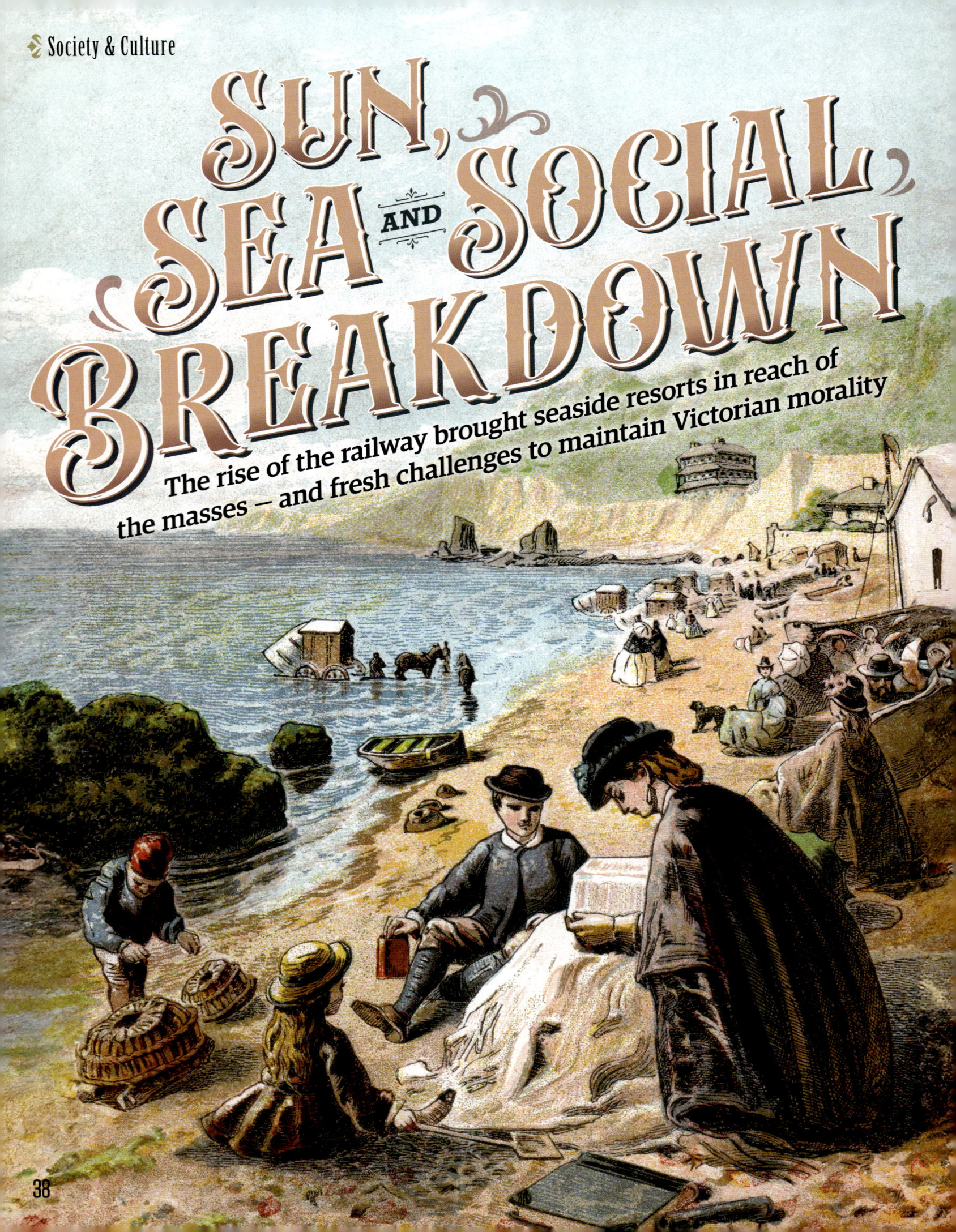

Sun, Sea and Social Breakdown

Women's swimsuits were designed to protect modesty

A photograph of Margate, Kent, taken circa 1900. The Victorian era saw it become home to an amusement park that later evolved into Dreamland, which still stands today

From sandcastles to fish and chips, promenades to pleasure piers, many of the things best associated with a trip to the British seaside have their roots in the Victorian summer holiday. However, while we take these seaside attractions for granted now – even looking back on them as old fashioned – many of them were considered revolutionary at the time, some even an affront to common decency. This led to some puritanical restrictions, but not even Victorian morality could hold back the tide of change that was rolling in.

PEACOCKING ON THE PROM

Trips to the seaside were nothing new at the beginning of the Victorian era, at least for the upper classes. In fact, 'taking the waters' for your health was so popular during the Georgian period that Jane Austen featured both the spa town of Bath in two of her novels and the coastal town of Lyme Regis in *Persuasion*. As Austen was keen to point out, while these trips were ostensibly about getting fresh air and exercise, they were also often an excuse for high society to mingle and show off. As well as prove that they could afford not to work, they could also stay at grand hotels, attend the theatre, and wear the latest fashions at parties.

A classic example of this exhibitionism masquerading as healthy living was promenading. A stroll along the seafront was considered good for the constitution, but a long, level 'prom' or esplanade was also like a public catwalk where you could be 'seen' by society and enjoy admiring glances as you strolled serenely by, decked out in your best attire. Promenading only grew in popularity during the Victorian era, with the first piers being built in the 1850s to give tourists somewhere to stroll as well as to moor ships.

While spa towns like Bath and Harrogate still held their appeal during Queen Victoria's reign, doctors were increasingly recommending trips to seaside resorts. This was mainly because they believed that the bracing sea air contained what they termed as 'ozone' or 'activated oxygen',

> "COASTAL TOWNS OFFERED A WELCOME BREAK FROM THE CHOKING POLLUTION"

something that was "very essential but also a preventative of disease and a great aid for the treatment of ailments of all character."

Prince Albert, a staunch advocate of science and healthy living, led by example by building a new royal residence by the sea in 1845: Osborne House on the Isle of Wight. The royal family spent many summers from July to August at their palatial holiday home, with Queen Victoria continuing to stay there regularly long after Albert died in 1861.

However, we now know that the Victorians were quite wrong about the seaside offering so-called activated oxygen. But in an era of rapidly industrialising towns and cities, it's likely that these coastal towns offered a welcome break from the choking pollution.

But the smog-ridden Industrial Revolution also brought railways. This new mode of transport could whisk you across country in a matter of hours, shrinking time itself and opening up a whole new world of endless opportunities of how people could spend their precious leisure time.

Although expensive, the burgeoning Victorian middle class could afford rail fares and were keen to follow en masse where the aristocrats led.

ALL ABOARD THE BATHING MACHINES

Up until the 1850s, it was not unusual for men to bathe or even swim in the sea completely naked. But such a tradition would not fit with the ever-expanding popularity of the seaside holiday. Not only were there more people sharing the beach, many of them were now women and children. Victorian values and correctness dictated that the proper etiquette was followed.

For example, as popular as promenading was, an unmarried woman was chaperoned by a married lady – a family member or friend – when strolling to ensure that the strict social boundaries between the sexes were not crossed and to ward off any unwanted or unsavoury advances. On the beach, this became something of a nightmare for Victorian decency, especially when it came to the tricky subject of bathing in the sea.

Promoted as a healthy pastime, sea bathing was as popular with Victorian women as men,

39

Society & Culture

A Victorian caricature showing ladies employing 'dippers' to help them get into the water

The amusement park on Tynemouth Sands in Tyne and Wear, circa 1900

> "BATHING MACHINES ALSO PLAYED A SMALL PART IN GIVING A CERTAIN LEVEL OF FREEDOM"

if not more so as it represented another small yet significant change in attitudes towards what women should and should not do. It is important to point out, however, that it was bathing in the sea that was the draw — swimming in open water was quite rare. Paddling and dipping were both thought to invigorate health, but the big question was how could men and women benefit from such pleasurable pursuits while maintaining the essential Victorian decorum?

The first solution was quite straightforward — men and women would bathe in separate parts of the beach. In 1847, Parliament gave local councils new powers to set how far apart the sexes had to be when bathing. One such by-law passed by Lowecroft, Suffolk, which was not unusual for the era, dictated: "A person of the female sex shall not, while bathing, approach within 100 yards of any place at which any person of the male sex, above the age of 12 years, may be set down for the purpose of bathing."

Regulation also required that women wore a "suitable gown or other sufficient dress or covering to prevent indecent exposure of the body." This swimwear could be extremely heavy; sometimes weights were even sown into it, so that dresses did not float to the surface. In choppy waters, these heavy outfits could drown a wearer. But these coveralls did serve another purpose: they stopped the ladies getting a suntan. Until the 1920s, having a tan was considered vulgar and only for workers in the fields. On the beach, parasols would also be employed to shade them from the sun.

However, as modest as Victorian swimwear was, to their prudish minds, a woman having to walk the length of the beach to the sea — even on a gender-segregated beach — was the equivalent of a modern 'walk of shame'. Instead, they used a bathing machine.

Strictly speaking, bathing machines dated back to around the 1750s and were not really 'machines'. Resembling a beach hut with four wheels, it would be rolled out to sea, usually pulled by horses. Some machines were equipped with a canvas tent around the doorway, capable of being lowered to the water and thus giving the bather greater privacy.

Once deep enough in the surf, the bather would then exit the cart using the door that was facing away from prying eyes on the beach and proceed to paddle. For inexperienced swimmers — which would have been most Victorian women in their billowing swimwear — some beach resorts offered the service of a 'dipper', a strong woman who would escort the bather out to sea in the cart and lift them into the water and yank them out when they were done. When the swimmer wanted the bathing machine brought back in, they would signal the operator by raising a small flag attached to the contraption's roof.

Bathing machines were deeply hypocritical. Men just strolled into the water wearing a considerably tighter swimsuit. But in a strange way, bathing machines also played a small part in giving a modicum of freedom to Victorian women, allowing them the privacy to experience sea bathing first-hand rather than be excluded altogether as they had been from so many other leisure activities and sports.

Another addition to the crowds that set the seaside holiday apart from anything that had gone before were children. Depending on class and standing in the world, Victorian children were either the educated future of the family line or just another worker, toiling in appalling conditions. But with rising prosperity came more disposable income and the ability to spend some time together as a family at the seaside. Those who once could only look on in admiration from afar as their 'betters' enjoyed a seaside break were now able to taste it for themselves.

As access to the seaside increased, many organised trips through churches, charities and societies such as the Temperance Movement gave opportunities to even the lowest in society. 1871 saw the introduction of the Bank Holidays Act that set aside four days through the year as official holidays for all for the first time. These were not paid — an entitlement to paid holiday would not become law until the 20th century — but with ever-improving transport links and the cost of an excursion subsidised by groups and organisations, the nature of the seaside holiday began to change dramatically both in its scale and its experience.

RESORTS BOOM
The railways transformed small communities - which often started as mere fishing villages - into bustling resorts to which people flocked in growing numbers.

Sun, Sea and Social Breakdown

THE GREAT COVER-UP
The modest way to take the air or take the plunge!

BATHING MACHINES
Invented to preserve the modesty of Victorian ladies, they would be pushed or pulled into the water either by men or a horse. The occupant could then descend the steps into the water with as little bodily 'exposure' as possible. Assistants could also be hired to help you into the water and 'take a dip' rather than swim, then aid you in returning up the steps.

A WHITER SHADE OF PALE
At first shaded bonnets, and then later less formal straw hats, were acceptable to keep the sun from colouring the face, which was not socially acceptable. Tanning was not fashionable until the 1920s.

THE HEADS-UP ON SENSIBLE BATHING
With a variety of styles, a hat or bonnet kept the hair neatly in place and covered. A dip up to the chest was all that was required and your head going under the water was very unladylike!

A SECOND LINE OF DEFENCE
If your hat or bonnet didn't give enough protection from the sun, a parasol did the trick. It was also very useful to shield you from the eyes of the lower classes and to hide telling blushes when being courted.

THE NECKLINE BEGINS TO TAKE THE PLUNGE
The high-buttoned collars of earlier swimwear gave way to a more relaxed approach. The blouse was still buttoned up for warmth and modesty, but it offered a feminine style with a belt that brought the outfit in at the waist.

CHIN UP TO KEEP OUT THE CHILL
A high-collared jacket was essential to remaining poised and keeping the sea breeze from causing a chill. It also protected the arms from the sun and insects. Elaborate lace would complete the feminine touch.

A LITTLE SKIN BEGINS TO APPEAR
Far more relaxed and braver, these sleeves gave exposure to both sea and sun, creating a little more freedom of movement and looking quite risqué. Sleeves would eventually creep further up the arms, but not for some time yet.

UNDER WRAPS FROM PRYING EYES AND PESTS
Necessary to cover the legs and the ankles from insects and gentlemen's gazes, long skirts were often paired with a crinoline petticoat to give it shape and a bustle at the rear — not easy for sitting in a deck chair! Lighter cotton skirts were introduced later.

AVOID SAND BETWEEN YOUR TOES AT ALL COSTS
Whether walking on the beach or the promenade, it was always wise to be prepared with a stout pair of shoes or boots, laced properly so as not to expose the ankles.

WEIGHED DOWN BY THE NEED FOR MODESTY
Trousers or skirts were a point of style and preference in heavy woollen material. Ladies often chose a combination of these, even putting weights into the over-skirt to stop it rising to the surface and exposing the trousers beneath.

YOU NEVER KNOW WHAT YOU MIGHT TREAD ON
Sea bathing did not involve swimming and so shoes or boots covered the ankles for modesty and were required when you stood in the water, in case of jagged pebbles or unspeakable sea creatures that may have been underfoot.

Society & Culture

ENTERTAINMENT FOR ALL
Typical scenes from the Victorian seaside

THE PROMENADE
A combination of exercise and showing off, 'promenading' was a chance to take in the sea air, meet friends and make a fashion statement. Unattached or unmarried young ladies and girls were chaperoned at first, but it was later common for groups of both working class men and women on organised trips to use a stroll along 'the prom' to meet and flirt.

ICE CREAM
Just one example of how the social taboo of eating outdoors was broken. A famous Victorian cook, Agnes Marshall, claimed to have invented her own freezer equipment, patented an ice cream maker and created the first ice cream cone. Ice cream sellers would push carts up and down the beach all day. Other street foods of the day were cockles, mussels and the very first fish and chips.

PUNCH AND JUDY
While this slapstick puppet show about an anarchic clown and his family is from 16th-century Italy, it became a British seaside attraction in the early 1800s. This was partly thanks to new mobile booths that the operator could quickly dismantle to search for new audiences. To suit Victorian tastes, Punch's old adversary, the devil, was replaced with a crocodile and his mistress, Pretty Polly, ceased to be included at all.

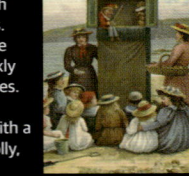

DONKEY RIDES
Rising in popularity in the latter part of the 19th century, these rides possibly evolved from the working donkeys that originally carried baskets of cockles and other shellfish as part of the local industry that supplied street vendors, hotels and boarding houses. Primarily for children, it was nevertheless enjoyed equally by adults, and in some areas, carts pulled by goats were also popular.

BANDSTAND
Victorians were well used to listening to bands playing in the open air at one of the many public parks that had sprung up around the country, and this outdoor entertainment was adopted to give an uplifting and invigorating atmosphere and entertainment to a day out by the sea.

BUILDING SANDCASTLES
As a means of keeping children entertained on the beach, buckets and spades were mass-produced from thin sheet metal and often brightly painted with decorations depicting the resort or scenes of a beach. Once purchased, they would be used year after year and were a popular and relatively cheap entertainment along with nets for exploring rock pools.

PLEASURE PALACES
The pier was both an extension of the promenade and a focal point for entertainment. This could be simply a selection of machines (later slot machines or 'one armed bandits') and a hall of mirrors so that crowds could experience being away from the shore and keeping their feet dry. The larger piers developed live music halls and concerts — and some even had their own train.

DECKCHAIRS
The concept of sunbathing was foreign to the Victorians, but they did recognise the benefits of sitting out in the open air, so it's no surprise that folding deckchairs were patented in the US in 1855. Originally used on ocean liners and steamships — hence the reference to a 'deck' — the transition to using the lightweight, highly portable chairs on beaches in port towns must have been a natural one.

Bathing machines line the beach front at Hastings, East Sussex, circa 1900

Bathing machines were necessary for women who wished to take a dip in the sea

PIER PRESSURE
Seaside towns sought to attract tourists by building ever longer piers

NORTH PIER, BLACKPOOL
Designed by Eugenius Birch, work began in 1862 and was completed in 1863. The pier was damaged in 1867 by Lord Nelson's former flagship, Foudroyant, which was moored alongside the pier as part of an exhibition. In the 1870s, the pierhead was enlarged and the Indian Pavilion and bandstand were built. There were further collisions with the pier from shipping in 1892 and 1897.

BRIGHTON
A relatively late construction, work began in 1891 and was completed in 1899. A tramway had been built to help with construction, but this was dismantled upon completion of the project. A 1,500-seat theatre was incorporated into the pierhead in 1901 along with various other smaller pavilions at various points along the construction.

LLANDUDNO
Designed by James Brunlees, construction began in 1876 and was completed in 1877. A number of additions followed, including a bandstand at the pier head in 1877 and a pavilion at the shore end in 1884 that also incorporated a swimming pool. Further construction in 1884 took it to its final length.

RYDE
The very first of its kind in the country, its location on the Isle of Wight close to Queen Victoria's summer retreat made it a popular destination. First opened in 1814, it underwent various extensions to its length and to the size of the pierhead, including the addition of a tramway alongside the pedestrian pier.

| 500 metres | 536.5 metres | 699.5 metres | 702.6 metres |

By the middle of the 19th century, towns such as Brighton had already expanded, numbering 44,000 in the 1841 census. Other popular resorts like Blackpool and Llandudno had started much smaller, but with the industrial centres of Manchester and the Midlands not far away, they rapidly turned into the must-go places for groups of friends and co-workers looking for a few hours of fun.

In response to such high demand and the ability of some holidaymakers to even stay for a night or two, accommodation became a valuable commodity. A range of boarding houses and hotels sprang up to suit every budget. Resorts that regarded themselves as catering for the better class of person — places like Brighton with its royal links to the Georgian era and Ryde on the Isle of Wight, with its proximity to Queen Victoria's Osborne House — tended to already have large, grand hotels as close to the seafront as possible.

But for Blackpool and similar destinations, the lack of deeply rooted tradition meant they had more freedom and could virtually start from scratch. Boarding houses and small hotels became booming businesses, but one rule applied no matter where you stayed: the closer to the sea, the higher the price. And unscrupulous landlords were always looking for ways of extracting as much out of people's pockets as they could by whatever means necessary — especially what was meant by a 'sea view'!

With the development of the resorts came the expansion of the wealth of the towns and what they were able to offer in entertainment for holidaymakers to spend their money on. In many cases, the local pier would be extended to become even more impressive, offering a greater variety of entertainment than before.

Building was sometimes on a grand scale, with the creation of much more indoor entertainment to combat the unpredictable British weather. Aquariums, amusement arcades, ballrooms and even circuses were constructed as permanent fixtures to keep the public entertained and keep them spending. With typical Victorian enterprise and invention, technology and mechanisation had their parts to play even amid the all-natural allure of the seaside. Electric lighting illuminated the promenade, steam carousels and fairground rides appeared on the prom and the pier. Competing resorts made bold statements to attract customers, and what better way than with a replica of the Eiffel Tower at Blackpool to embody a sense of pride and success? The beach had not been forgotten — it was now just part of the whole drama and no longer the main character. What had been created for the seaside break was more choice and less reason to leave.

From rather sedate, genteel beginnings at the start of the Victorian age, by the end of the 19th century things were starting to look somewhat different. As the era progressed, so did the resorts, expanding not only in size but in what they had to offer. Demand drove innovation not only in the construction of new entertainments but also in transport, with rapid improvement of the railway network to help quench the ever-popular thirst to get away from it all.

People from all walks of life now shared the experience and attitudes, and standards slowly started to change. Many traditional ladies would still not take a dip in the sea, but for a younger, more liberal generation, it was a release from the strict ties of social boundaries that they fully embraced. Ladies' swimwear become slightly less restrictive and more risqué; the sexes mixed openly on the prom; bawdy 'what the butler saw' machines appeared in the arcades; and comedians told rude jokes in the music halls.

Tired of increasingly having to mix with the hoi polloi, the upper classes began to abandon their traditional resorts. Instead they spent their time and money on foreign holidays where, for now at least, the masses could not follow. What was left were the majority who had learned how to relax and enjoy themselves, willing and able to spend their hard-earned cash on a dazzling array of entertainments.

It was the working man and his family who had taken ownership of the seaside holiday. With ever-improving conditions for workers, the popularity of what the Victorians created continued to rise, leaving a legacy that still rings true today — and it is them we must thank that even now we all still love to be beside the seaside.

A young couple frolic in the foreground while others enjoy the sands at Yarmouth beach, taken in 1895

"STANDARDS SLOWLY STARTED TO CHANGE"

SOUTHPORT
The local corporation first made plans for a pier in 1840, but it was not until 1859 that work began. It was designed by James Brunlees and first opened in 1860. Developments over the years have seen waiting rooms for boat passengers added, the pier lengthened and widened and a tramway built. A further extension in 1868 brought it to its final length.

1,107 metres

SOUTHEND
The longest pleasure pier in the world, it was originally built in 1829 as an attraction for visitors from London and extends out into the Thames estuary. The wooden pier was only 180 metres long when first opened, but it was extended over time and by 1848 was already the longest pier in Europe.

2,158 metres

Society & Culture

Wakes Week

When everyone in town went off on holiday together

Written by Edoardo Albert

Life for mill workers in Lancashire mill towns was tough. By the early 20th century, however, conditions had improved significantly; Elk Mill in Oldham, which was built in 1927, was the last Lancashire mill to be constructed and its 380 employees worked a 45-hour week, from 7.30am to 5.30pm. This was much better than the 12-hour days of the early Victorian era. Elk Mill was one of the best employers and it kept spinning until 1998. However, it was still hard, dirty, noisy work from which any holiday was a godsend.

It was, it turned out, God's friends, the saints, who instituted the holidays that mill workers came to enjoy during the early 20th century, holidays that turned Blackpool into the seaside resort it became.

In medieval times, when people lived in villages, each village church would celebrate the feast of the saint it was named after. Many of the saints to whom northern churches were dedicated, such as St Mary (15 August), St John (24 June) and saints Peter and Paul (29 June) happened to have their feast days in the summer. As part of the festival, villagers would hold a vigil in the church on the night before the feast – a wake – and then in the morning carry fresh rushes into the church to replace those that had covered the floor for the last year. Then, after a church service, there was feasting, fun and games and so much general merrymaking that, of course, the Puritans banned the custom during the Commonwealth.

Charles II reinstituted the custom following the Restoration. However, following the Industrial Revolution, as people moved from villages into new industrial towns, the custom of Wakes Week shifted towards a secular holiday. People from a town took a week off work – unpaid but desperately needed – and headed down the railway to holiday destinations, particularly the seaside towns of the north west, such as Blackpool, Morecambe and Southport.

Unable to stop their workers doing this, the mill owners decided to use the week to carry out maintenance on the factory. However, to ensure that Blackpool and the other resorts were not overwhelmed, a rota was developed, so that each town took its week at a different time during the summer. The whole town decamped to the seaside for the week, sharing holiday accommodation and spending, in one wild holiday splurge, all the money carefully saved during the year for Wakes Week.

School holidays, particularly in Lancashire, were staggered to take account of Wakes Week until relatively recently: the standardisation of the school year was the final blow to the old custom.

Wakes Week

Donkey rides on the beach at Blackpool were some of the key childhood memories for people who went on Wakes Week

BOLTON HOLIDAYS.

A NEW KIND of HOLIDAY!

TAKE OUT A

"WAKES WEEK" HOLIDAY CONTRACT TICKET

AVAILABLE MONDAY TO FRIDAY

YOU CAN
- Visit different places of interest each day!
- Visit the same place each day!
- Break your journey at intermediate Stations!
- Stay overnight if you wish!

AT A VERY CHEAP RATE!

ASK AT THE BOOKING OFFICE FOR PARTICULARS

BE A CONTRACT HOLDER ON YOUR HOLIDAYS!

With so many people travelling, railway companies offered different types of tickets, including this one that allowed people to make day trips to the coast rather than staying there overnight

Holidaymakers arriving in Blackpool, pushing their luggage on a trolley. Note how smartly everyone is dressed

"THE MILL OWNERS DECIDED TO USE THE WEEK TO CARRY OUT MAINTENANCE ON THE FACTORY"

Image source: Getty

Society & Culture

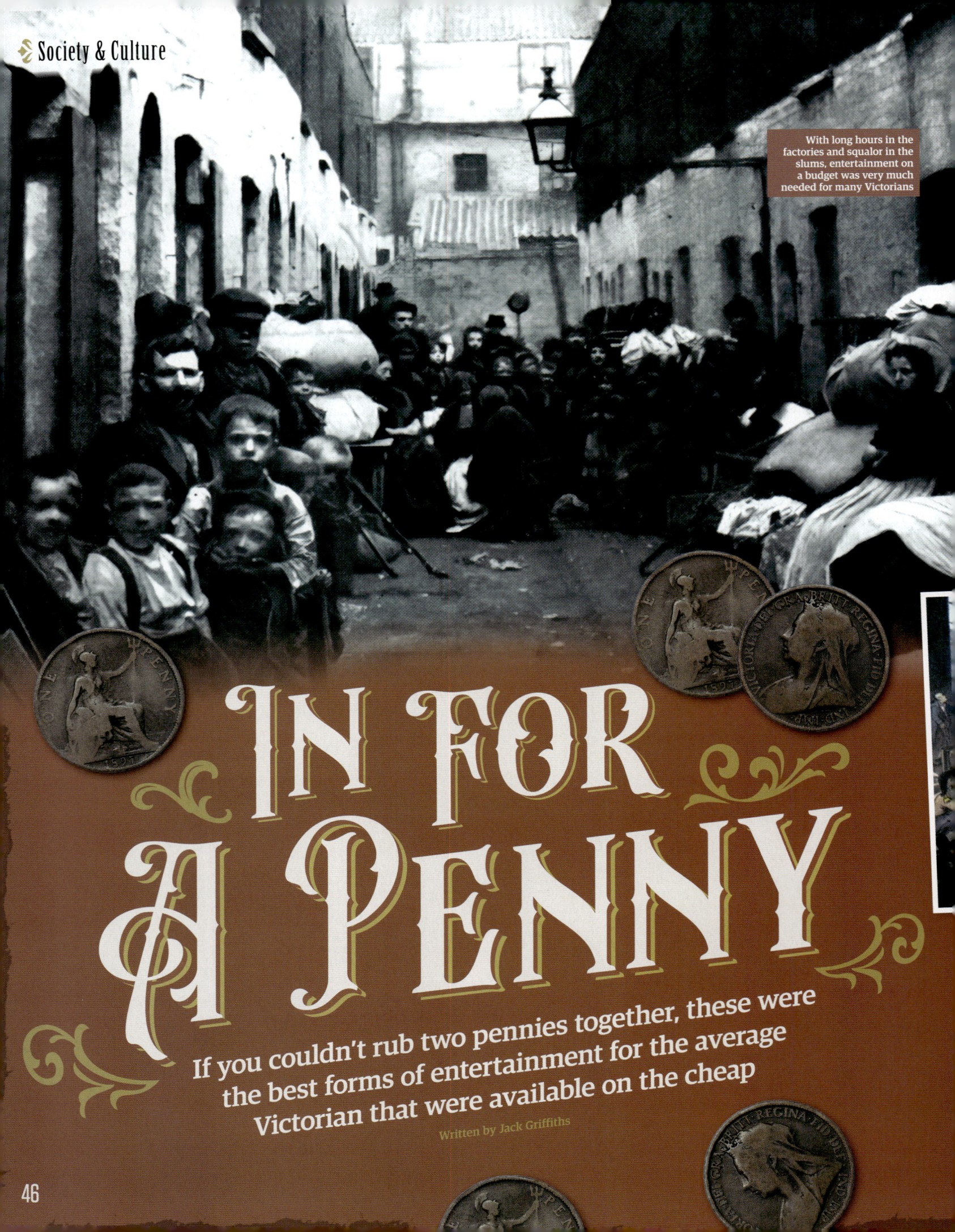

With long hours in the factories and squalor in the slums, entertainment on a budget was very much needed for many Victorians

In For A Penny

If you couldn't rub two pennies together, these were the best forms of entertainment for the average Victorian that were available on the cheap

Written by Jack Griffiths

In For A Penny

The Industrial Revolution had overseen the creation of vast numbers of jobs in the city, but it couldn't be all work and no play. After a long shift at the factory or mill, people wanted to let off some steam before the grind began anew the next day. However, low wages meant that there wasn't much of a salary to spend on having fun. And so the art of cheap entertainment was born. These pastimes, games and activities offered people an escape route to temporarily forget the hardships of working at a mill, for the cost of not much more than a penny.

Few of the working class could afford a day at a museum or a night at the theatre. Instead, the order of the day was a cheap cuisine or even a good book. Of particular excitement were the cheap thrills of the penny gaffs. Many were taken in by the promise of wonder deployed by showmen who called the shots. A famous showman who orchestrated many events was Tom Norman. The former butcher's assistant was one of the most famous freak show ringleaders and opened 13 penny gaffs around London, as the desire for cheap entertainment showed no signs of fading.

The popularity of penny reading helped build interest in arts and literature

PENNY READING

Penny readings certainly offered bang for your buck. Taking place in a small venue, this form of entertainment was particularly beneficial for those that were illiterate, as books and newspapers were read aloud. This enabled more of the population to discover current affairs and to expand their knowledge of both news and literature. Of course, before everybody went home, there was also just time for a quick rendition of the national anthem.

Cock fighting drew in the crowds who could make some quick cash

THE DEPRAVITY OF COCK FIGHTING

This horrific pastime was popular in the Victorian era. In fact, the name 'penny gaff' originates here, with 'penny' describing the cost and 'gaff' the shape of the fighting pits. As for the activity, people bet on which chicken would win in a fight. The longer it lasted, the rowdier the crowd became. A bloodthirsty endeavour, it was popular long before the Victorians but, thankfully, virtually ended in Britain under the Cruelty to Animals Act in 1849.

The penny sit-up can be seen as a predecessor of homeless shelters

PENNY SIT-UP

Sleeping on the streets was an all too common sight in Victorian cities as accommodation was often too inadequate or too pricey. Penny sit-ups provided the homeless with just a little bit extra to help them through the night. For a penny, you could hire a bench to sit on in a small shelter for the night and, for a few pennies more, this could be upgraded to a comfy wooden coffin to lie down in.

47

Society & Culture

THE 'WONDERS' OF THE FREAK SHOW

A repulsive pastime, the freak show was nevertheless a popular event. The shows promised rare sights that would shock the audience, from the 'pig-faced lady' to the 'elephant man'. To add to the spectacle, these people would be given elaborate back stories that would be told by the showman upon their unveiling to the audience. In reality, behind the curtain these were simply people with deformities or abnormalities who were likely unable to work and simply exploited to make money. The shows travelled around different cities across the country and remained popular throughout the 19th century.

By the end of the 19th century public opinion had shifted and freak shows were seen as distasteful

The Mutoscope
For Pennies   A Moving Picture Machine

Size, 4 feet, 8 inches high.   Shipping weight, 325 pounds

Pop a penny into the machine and enjoy the show at the penny arcade

ALL THE FUN OF THE PIER

Away from the hustle and bustle of the crowded cities, there was lots of fun to be had at the beach. Seaside towns prospered with the advent of the train, which allowed people to travel to the coast, quickly. On the pier were a number of penny arcade machines where you could simply pop a coin in and enjoy the show. Gamble your earnings away on a one-armed bandit slot machine, be wowed by moving models like the laughing sailor, or turn a hand crank and enjoy a brief silent film reel flipbook at your leisure.

PILLS AND POTIONS

There was also a dark side to life outside of the workhouse. With little to no drug regulation in the first half of the 19th century in particular, cheap concoctions could be picked-up at a nearby chemist. Cocaine and opium were available in shops and at markets, brought into Britain from all corners of the empire. The drugs were used to make home remedies to try and alleviate symptoms of a poor diet and lifestyle.

The sale of harmful drugs decreased after the 1868 Pharmacy Act and then the 1920 Dangerous Drugs Act

In For A Penny

Street musicians including a tin-whistler

WHISTLE WHILE YOU (DON'T) WORK

Pianos, violins and harps were strictly for the richest in society but what about a tin whistle? Known as a penny whistle for its budget price, this flute-like instrument was quite simple to play too – just blow into the mouthpiece while covering one or more of the holes and enjoy the different sounds. Mass-produced due to the readily-available amounts of tin in Britain, they were a popular instrument used in street music by both children and adults.

TUCK IN TO FANCY CUISINE

Those bored of a staple diet of bread, butter and potatoes could stretch their earnings for something a bit fancier. Onions, leeks and watercress cost less than a penny and were amongst the healthier options available. If you fancied some meat on your plate, but couldn't afford the prime cuts, jellied eels were popular in London's East End or a butcher would happily part with a slink (a cow foetus), or even a pig's head.

Only the wealthier in Victorian society could afford good quality meat

LOSE YOURSELF IN A PENNY DREADFUL

An escape route from the monotonous boredom of the factory was the penny dreadful. These adventure books were available in eight episodes, each costing a penny. Sensational and gory, they, perhaps, weren't the greatest examples of literature, but were a fun and exciting read nonetheless. Penny dreadfuls were of particular interest to working class boys and formed a big part of popular culture. Although violent, they detailed grand adventures across the world in cities and environments unknown to much of British society or voyages into the future and journeys back into the past.

If you couldn't afford a penny for the escapist fiction, then the books would be circulated on the streets and in schools. Not liked by all, some blamed them for encouraging violence, especially after the murder of Emily Coombs in London in 1895, where a collection of penny dreadfuls were found in the perpetrators' house.

Violent and often gruesome, the penny dreadful nonetheless was a break from an often bleak reality

SPEND A PENNY

Chaotic workhouses and small, unhygienic homes meant a clean toilet was not always available. If you had a spare penny though, you could spend it at a public restroom. The idea was first demonstrated at the 1851 Great Exhibition and helped clean the streets of human waste. Many were also built in underground tunnels to provide more space on street level. These toilets were first only for men and it wasn't until 1889 that the first female public toilets opened in London, as a place for women in the fashionable West End to have a break in between shopping trips.

The phrase 'spend a penny' originates from the cheap cost of a public toilet

49

TURN TO THE WALL, GIRL!

The rules that Victorian servants were expected to follow

Written by Edoardo Albert

Life below stairs was tough, but it was still better than most of the alternatives. In 1901, at the end of the Victorian era, the national census recorded 1.3 million people as domestic servants, second only to agricultural workers as a sector of the population. Domestic servants worked in a huge variety of homes, from vast country estates with hundreds of staff to a single maid living in the attic of a house in the new railway suburbs. Hours were long, holidays few and the only time off was the weekly trip to church and, if they had indulgent employers, a single free afternoon.

The work day stretched from 6am, when servants woke to light fires, trim lanterns and prepare breakfast, to 10pm. With servants living in the same house and sharing much the same space as the family they worked for, detailed rules to delineate servant from master were required. Generally, it was the job of experienced servants to train new members of the household but there was also a brisk trade in handbooks for the mistresses of Victorian households, telling them how to manage their staff.

The rules themselves varied by household. Even in the most relaxed homes, however, the demarcation between upstairs and downstairs was marked. Some of the stricter instruction manuals enjoined the Victorian mistress to impose rules that included telling housemaids to turn their faces to the wall when a lady or gentleman passed them in a corridor. That, however, was generally regarded as a bit extreme: in most houses, it was considered sufficient for the servant to simply back against the wall while allowing the quality to pass.

The Servant's Behaviour Book, or, Hints on Manners and Dress for Maid Servants in Small Households by Emily Augusta Patmore, published in 1859, is typical of the manuals of the time. In it, Mrs Patmore enjoins servants to "Never let your voice be heard by the ladies or gentlemen of the house except when necessary, and then as little as possible." After all, as Mrs Patmore explained to her servant readers: "Ladies have been educated in a very different manner to you. They have read many books, have travelled and seen many sights, talked with educated people, and know a great number of things about which you know nothing. It is not likely that you can have anything to say that will amuse or interest a lady. When she talks to you, it is in kindness, and all the pleasure of the talk is on your side."

Mrs Patmore died from tuberculosis at 38, leaving a family of six children. In Victorian England, death was the great disrespector of social standing.

Despite her views on her social inferiors, Emily Patmore was not a petit bourgeois but a member of the artistic circle that produced the Pre-Raphaelites: this portrait of her is by John Everett Millais

"THERE WAS A BRISK TRADE IN HANDBOOKS FOR THE MISTRESSES OF HOUSEHOLDS"

This photograph makes clear just how young girls were when they started as domestic servants

Cleaning took up much of the day for domestic servants and it all had to be done by hand: there were no labour-saving devices

Society & Culture

Conspicuous Consumption

The limited understanding of disease in the Victorian era created a number of unusual fashions which saw the healthy envying the sick

Written by Ben Gazur

Conspicuous Consumption

The wan and pale figure of a woman suffering from tuberculosis became the epitome of attractiveness for many Victorians

In Puccini's 1895 opera La bohème the character of Mimi succumbs to tuberculosis at the end of the action, despite the kindness of her friends

At the beginning of the Victorian period science was making amazing advances in chemistry, physics and technology, but medicine lagged behind in a number of ways. Though bacteria had been discovered in the 17th century there was still no understanding that they were the causative agents of many illnesses. Disease seemed to strike victims almost at random or was simply the will of God, and doctors could often do little for their patients.

One of the primary theories about sickness was that it was spread by miasma – bad and polluted airs associated with rotting biological matter. There is some sense in this as unclean and unhygienic areas are often sources of infection. Miasma theory had dominated European ideas of illness since antiquity and still captured the minds of many. It was also expanded outside of disease to explain other aspects of biology. In 1844 one professor wrote that it is "from inhaling the odour of beef the butcher's wife obtains her obesity."

Victorian cities were certainly malodorous places at the best of times. Since the late 18th century more and more people were congregating in cities as that was where jobs were being created in factories. London's population in 1800 was around 2 million, but by the end of the century it was nearly 7 million. Housing for the poor – the majority of the population – became ever more cramped and created the perfect conditions for the rapid spread of diseases. The infrastructures of cities were not able to cope with the demands placed on them and the government was unwilling to pay for creating them. In such conditions epidemics of cholera, typhus, and smallpox were common events.

In 1858 London was struck by a warm summer which turned the River Thames, used as a sewer at the time, into such a reeking watercourse that the event was known as The Great Stink. Parliament could not ignore the calls for reform of the sewage system – they could not even open their windows because they let in such a foul aroma. If smells created sickness then London was doomed.

By the later years of the Victorian era there was a far better understanding of how diseases were caused but social stigma was still attached to certain ailments. Cholera was linked to poverty and dirty living, syphilis was tied to loose morals, and Chimney Sweeps' Scrotum (a cancer linked to soot) was found mainly in those who worked up chimneys from a young age. But if there were diseases to look down on there were also diseases which some people aspired to contract. Fashionable diseases were one of the stranger fads among the Victorians.

CONSUMPTIVE CHIC

Humans are strange creatures. When one person of a high status does something, others who wish to be associated with that status will emulate it and this includes their illnesses. Princess Alexandra of Denmark, wife to the future Edward VII, inspired a number of fashions thanks to her history of sickness. She often wore high chokers to conceal

53

Society & Culture

The fact that up to a quarter of all deaths were caused by tuberculosis did little to dissuade fashionable ladies from attempting to copy its symptoms

a scar on her neck, and so chokers came to be popular. When rheumatic fever left the princess with a limp, fashionable ladies copied it. Canny shoe-makers even sold shoes of different sizes to help ladies mimic the royal shuffle more easily.

But, there was one illness above all others which shaped Victorian fashion. Tuberculosis, known as consumption to the Victorians, is a bacterial disease which is spread through inhalation of air droplets when an infected person coughs, sneezes or even speaks – however, this was unknown at the time. To the Victorians, it was a particularly mysterious sickness as not everyone who is infected develops the symptoms of consumption. Those who did sicken suffered chest pains, tiredness, a bloody cough, and a slow wasting away. For some, these symptoms were irresistible.

Consumption was a disease which appealed to Romantic sensibilities. Victims of tuberculosis took on a waif-like appearance with pale skin, fine and silky hair, general thinness and prominent cheek bones. Even as their skin grew pallid their cheeks were often left rosy and their lips became blood red. Under their increasingly transparent flesh blue-blooded veins, associated with aristocracy, became visible. These were all common markers of beauty for the Victorians. It seemed as if the illness made people more attractive, even as it killed them. Charlotte Brontë, who watched her sisters die from the illness in the 1840s, wrote that "consumption, I am aware, is a flattering malady."

Because many tuberculosis patients did die young it made their lives seem to shine all the brighter. The fatigue caused by consumption made victims unable to do manual labour but left them, if they could afford it, the time to focus on arts and literature. Poets, authors, and painters who died young from tuberculosis held a grim glamour as they were perceived to have been cut off in their prime. In popular imagination, consumption was a disease of those with artistic tendencies. Too much mental exercise was thought to bring on consumption so those with tuberculosis became associated with genius.

Those with consumption were assumed to have very sensitive natures and deep emotions. Alexandre Dumas wrote: "It was the fashion to suffer from the lungs; everybody was consumptive, poets especially; it was good form to spit blood after each emotion that was at all sensational, and to die before reaching the age of thirty." The torpor

Conspicuous Consumption

Elizabeth Siddal, the model for John Everett Millais' painting Ophelia, suffered tuberculosis and her pale skin was considered one of her finest assets

> "THOSE WITH CONSUMPTION WERE ASSUMED TO HAVE SENSITIVE NATURES AND DEEP EMOTIONS"

of an ailing consumptive was thought to be very becoming to women in particular.

Consumptive patients alternated between periods of physical collapse and remission where they seemed to regain their health. When feeling healthy they could attend balls, go to dinners, and mingle with society. In these moments their beautiful malady was noted by other members of society and judged to be very appealing. The question became how to achieve this appearance for those unfortunate enough to remain stubbornly free of the disease.

Among those who cultivated consumptive chic there were a number of tricks available. Cosmetics allowed women to paint their faces to a suitable pallor though more extreme measures were available. Arsenic wafers, advertised as "perfectly harmless", could be eaten, and promised the effect of "producing, preserving and enhancing beauty of form and person in male and female by surely developing a transparency and pellucid clearness of complexion, shapely contour of form, brilliant eyes, soft and smooth skin." Arsenic poisoning may well do this, but it was also deadly. Men, on the whole, attempted to appear less consumptive as the fragility it created was antithetical to the Victorian ideas of virile masculinity.

Women wore corsets which emphasised their slender waists, and could also change their posture to make them look as if they were wilting under the pains of illness. The voluminous skirts favoured by Victorian ladies also served to underline just how thin they were. Weakness in ladies was prized as it showed they did not have to work and were not 'mannish' in their personality.

Perhaps one of the most enviable factors in consumption infections were the frequent trips which wealthy victims were encouraged to take to resorts with 'healthy airs'. Thousands of spas appeared across Europe to aid the recovery of the consumptive. High altitudes, sunny climates, and good diets were considered the best ways to improve health. They also made ideal holiday destinations and many would have envied the life enjoyed by wealthy consumptives. Those who could not afford to recuperated at such resorts could only dream of these luxurious conditions.

The art of the Victorians underlined the beauty and romance of contracting tuberculosis. The operas *La bohème* and *La traviata* both end with the deaths of pretty young women from consumption. Many of the models for some of the most famous images of the age were suffering from tuberculosis, such as Elizabeth Siddal who sat for many of the Pre-Raphaelite painters. Paintings of patients with consumption showed them passing away peacefully in bed surrounded by loved ones, which was thought of as the perfect death.

Fashions change however and the fad for tuberculosis ended as science advanced. In the 1880s it was determined that consumption was not caused by a sensitive soul but by the infectious germ mycobacterium tuberculosis. From then on tuberculosis was not something to be envied but something to be feared like any other illness. Those with consumption were to be pitied and were probably infected by their unsanitary living conditions. Radiant health became the epitome of beauty. Since it was also known that consumptives were now a danger to the healthy, sanatoriums were erected for the poor where they could be held together in one place without risk to the general public. In these institutions every moment of a patient's time was monitored and controlled. No one would envy these nasty and short lives.

BROAD STREET PUMP

How one Victorian doctor helped debunk the miasma theory

In 1854 a cholera outbreak struck the London area of Soho. Within a few weeks over 600 people were dead. Based on the miasma theory of disease it seemed likely that bad air was infecting the area, producing the epidemic. Doctor John Snow had already begun questioning whether there was another method of cholera infection which involved spreading the 'germ' of cholera between people. The outbreak in Soho gave him an opportunity to test his theory.

Through interviewing the people of Soho, Snow discovered that most of the infected drew their water from a pump on Broad Street. Snow's research was conclusive enough to convince the London authorities to remove the handle from the pump at the centre of the infection to prevent anyone else drinking the water. Instances of cholera in Soho soon dwindled. It was found that sewage from a nearby cesspit had been leaking into the water supply. Snow also noted that workers at a nearby brewery avoided infection as they drank beer made with boiled water.

Later statistical work carried out by Snow was able to prove that tainted water was the cause of the spread of cholera. With results such as these the miasma theory of infection became increasingly unlikely.

The work of Dr Snow on how cholera is spread has led to him being considered to be the Father of Epidemiology

Society & Culture

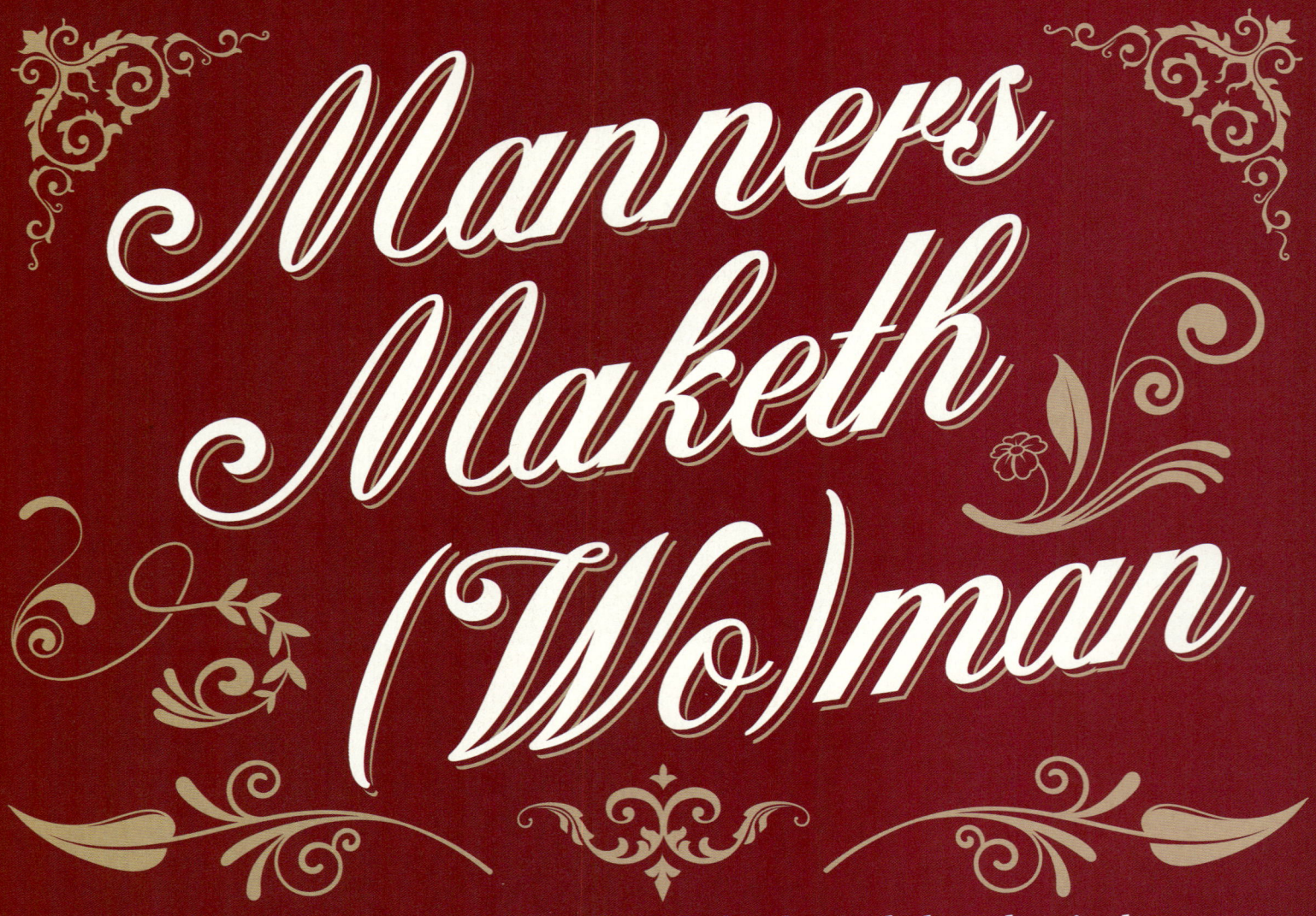

Manners Maketh (Wo)man

Follow an upper middle-class lady through her day in late Victorian England, a social minefield fraught with etiquette bombs primed to shame her, should she make the slightest misstep

Written by Ben Biggs

As befitting any lady of her station, Lady Darcy begins her day by taking a bath, applying her make-up in a routine kept secret even from her beloved, before her servants squeeze her into a corset and crinolette - a fashionable steel-framed dome that props up the rear of her dress. Naturally, there will be no callers before three o'clock at her townhouse in Mayfair, London, so she steps out to take the air in Green Park. Lord Darcy is at work in the stock exchange, so Lady Darcy goes happily unaccompanied: gone are her débutante days when she would have required a chaperone for such a venture.

The promenade is busy today and she acknowledges several gentlemen acquaintances, who return her greeting by lifting their hats, before she spies her good friend Lord Davenport walking in the opposite direction. She offers him her arm and Lord Davenport dutifully takes it, joining Lady Darcy on a short walk in the direction he just came from. So as not to cause a scene, they engage in suitably reticent conversation about the weather and the health of their spouses. Then Lord Davenport makes a polite excuse about a prior engagement, turns and strides off in the direction he was originally heading in.

Lady Darcy is home long before tea time, which gives her enough time to freshen up for her afternoon guest. Perhaps it's because Mr Brown is of new money and lower breeding that he arrives a full 15 minutes before three o'clock, talks far too liberally and leaves at half-past three, but there's no excuse for placing his hat and riding crop on the floor underneath his chair. Nevertheless, Lady Darcy wears a smile throughout this vulgar discourse, as Lord Darcy wishes to court Mr Brown for a lucrative investment.

That evening, Lord and Lady Darcy attend Earl Granby's dinner party. They arrive a fashionable 15 minutes late, which gives the Darcys time to admire the Duke of Bedford's calling card displayed prominently on the Earl's drawing room mantlepiece. The Darcys are the seventh couple in the dining room procession, preceded by several Barons, a Viscount and, of course, led by the Earl and countess themselves. Mercifully, no singletons are invited to complicate the procession or the seating arrangement, although Vicar Dibley frequently breaks protocol by speaking to his wife, who is sitting to his left instead of Lady Darcy on his right, which is quite rude and unexpected from a man of the cloth.

Manners Maketh (Wo)man

Dinner parties were an elaborate affair overstuffed with common sense rules (like not speaking with your mouth full) and esoteric laws of etiquette. Ladies and gentlemen were seated in an alternating arrangement and gentlemen were expected to speak largely to the lady the host had assigned to them

Victorians loved leaving calling cards: it was only proper for friends and acquaintances to arrange a visit with a card bearing their name

Ladies initiated greetings by offering their hand. Gentlemen were to briefly and gently take it with their right. Gentlemen meanwhile initiated greetings by lifting their hat with the hand farthest from the lady

A LEFT-HANDED COMPLIMENT.

"Back again, Doctor? I've been *so* much better since you went away!"

57

Society & Culture

Moral Outrage

Buttoned up, prudish and joyless, the Victorians have a reputation for prim and proper behaviour, but the reality was very different

Written by Catherine Curzon

Moral Outrage

When it comes to Victorian attitudes to sex, a popular and entirely spurious myth suggests that they were so averse to any suggestion of nakedness that they even covered the legs of their furniture. Though that isn't true, it perfectly sums up the legendarily prudish approach to sex that the Victorians adhered to.

In fact, it's a little more complex than that. Victorians weren't quite the puritans we might imagine, famed for preferring to lie back and think of England as they did the unthinkable deed.

THE BLUSHING BRIDE

Before Queen Victoria ascended to the throne in 1837, the Georgians had celebrated excess in all things, but everything changed in the new era. It was an age in which frowning morality replaced Georgian bawdiness. For morally strong women, thinking about sex before the wedding night was unthinkable and medical texts intended for men warned them that the very act of intercourse might be enough to terrify their blushing bride.

Women, wrote the medical gentlemen, were indifferent to sex at best and actively traumatised by it at worst. Having lived lives of purity, without a single lustful thought, it was up to the husband to ease his new wife into the realities of sex. After all, the textbooks warned, women would need sex if they were to have babies, and have babies was what women should do. Procreation was the only reason a lady would want to have sex, after all. It was all nonsense, of course.

However, sex within the Victorian marriage wasn't all miserable duty. Marriage guides from the era often explained that a woman who was in a sexually satisfying partnership was more likely to become pregnant. Indeed, they suggested that a female orgasm was just as important to conception as the male. There was room for passion, fun and love, not just passive grinding.

Whilst women were largely expected to remain pure in thought and deed until they were wives, it is a fiction that all Victorian husbands believed that their wives would not and should not be expected to enjoy sex. Victorian sex was rich with double standards in many other respects though and for men, it was a case of anything goes.

NORMAL SEX

As attitudes to sex grew more restrictive, the Victorians rationalised them as a natural response to overpopulation. Overpopulation was believed to be the cause of disease, poverty and feminine hysteria, and the more sex there was, the more children would be born. It was necessary, therefore, to regulate sex itself.

In order to do this, sex was put into two categories: normal and abnormal. The former was defined only as heterosexual sex between husband and wife. Anything beyond that was considered abnormal and deviant, from masturbation to pornography, or sex work to homosexuality. This, of course, made all of those things even more tempting.

YOUNG MEN ABOUT TOWN

Even as Victorian instructional texts were warning husbands that they must be understanding when

> For the Victorians, table legs weren't taboo, but a lot of other things were. Sex was a worrying word... and an even more worrying act

Society & Culture

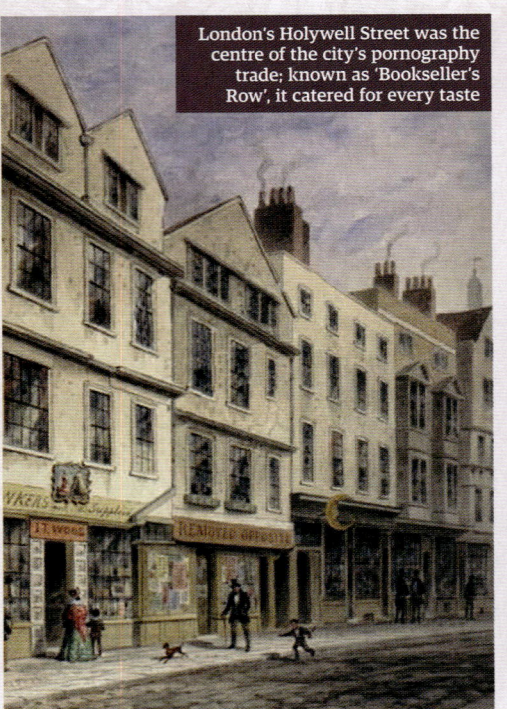

Elizabeth Siddal, muse of Pre-Raphaelite artist Dante Gabriel Rossetti, was one of the most celebrated and famed female artist's models

London's Holywell Street was the centre of the city's pornography trade; known as 'Bookseller's Row', it catered for every taste

Far from the image of the fallen woman, courtesans such as Catherine 'Skittles' Walters grew rich and celebrated, enjoying a coterie of admirers

it came to their wife's horror of sex, that wasn't the case when it came to men. Sex workers were simply assumed to be a rite of passage for young men and it was important, said the men in the know, that wives should not be expected to behave as sex workers did when it came to sex.

Whilst women were supposedly pure, it was believed that men were creatures who had to let off their sexual steam. Many did this in the brothels situated in cities or with sex workers elsewhere, of which there were thousands. Victorian crusaders offered help to these so-called fallen women, even as some of these self-same crusaders retired at night to flagellate themselves as punishment for their impure thoughts about the women.

PORNOGRAPHY

Even as open discussion of sex and sexuality in anything other than a medical sense was frowned upon, sex work and pornography found a flourishing market in the Victorian world. In fact, the suggestion that sex was in itself taboo lent an extra frisson to the act, whether it was with a lover, a sex worker or with the help of pornography. Consuming pornography alone was sinful in Victorian morality; after all, masturbation was just one more thing that came under the umbrella of abnormal sexuality.

Thanks to the proliferation of the mass printing press, Victorian smut was sometimes made in England, sometimes on the Continent; and for the connoisseur, it was often French. It was available to anyone who knew where to look, with the centre of the erotica industry in England located on Holywell Street. Contrary to the notion that women should not be expected to enjoy sex, but instead should consider it a marital duty in order to procreate, Victorian pornography often celebrated sexuality. In the black-and-white images produced and sold in the era, the women frequently look like they're having a great time.

Of course, there was a darker side to this pornography. Violence and rape were also depicted, as was imagery alluding to castration and the threat to men that sexually liberated women represented. Nowhere is this better represented than in the erotic novel, *The Lustful Turk*, in which a woman cuts off a man's penis as she achieves orgasm. Whilst this book was published during the reign of George IV, it didn't

> "MEN WERE CREATURES WHO HAD TO LET OFF THEIR SEXUAL STEAM"

achieve popular recognition until the Victorian era, when its publisher, William Dugdale, was cited as a producer of obscenity during the trial that led to the introduction of the Obscene Publications Act 1857.

Every kind of fetish was catered for and, in a world in which homosexuality was a crime, every sexual preference too. Of course, whilst there is a celebration to the act of sex in Victorian porn, it is also a world of lost chances and of hidden secrets: whilst the women in the photographs appear to be enjoying themselves, the people consuming the images might never see such pleasure in their actual lives. Likewise, those consuming homosexual pornography might never feel able to express their desires in reality for fear of persecution or far worse.

With pornography sales riding high, Lord Chief Justice, Lord Campbell, described the trade as "more deadly than [...] arsenic". As a result a controversial Obscene Publication Act was brought into being, intended to ban any work written with the aim of corrupting morality decency. It was a very Victorian sort of act, and it still exists today in an updated form.

ARTIST'S MODELS

Unsurprisingly, male and female artist's models had a very difference experience in the Victorian era. The male model represented perfection, physically and morally strong and the representation of peak maleness. Female models, however, were considered to be somewhere close to sex workers. Posing for male artists, they were subjected to and redrawn in the image of the male gaze, drawing audiences to look at the resultant works even as the women they represented were looked down upon.

Many of the models were working-class women and they were often looked down upon by the artists who drew them as morally or intellectually beneath them. As Victorian morality chased female models out of academies and into private studios, the air of vice that already hung around them without any reason grew even thicker. In fact, the reality was often far less thrilling and forbidden. Modelling could be unthinkable, thankless and cold; that it was also demonised was the final insult. After all, not every model could become a famous artist's muse and for those who were, social acceptance was rarely a side effect: the plaudits were usually reserved for those making the art instead.

Moral Outrage

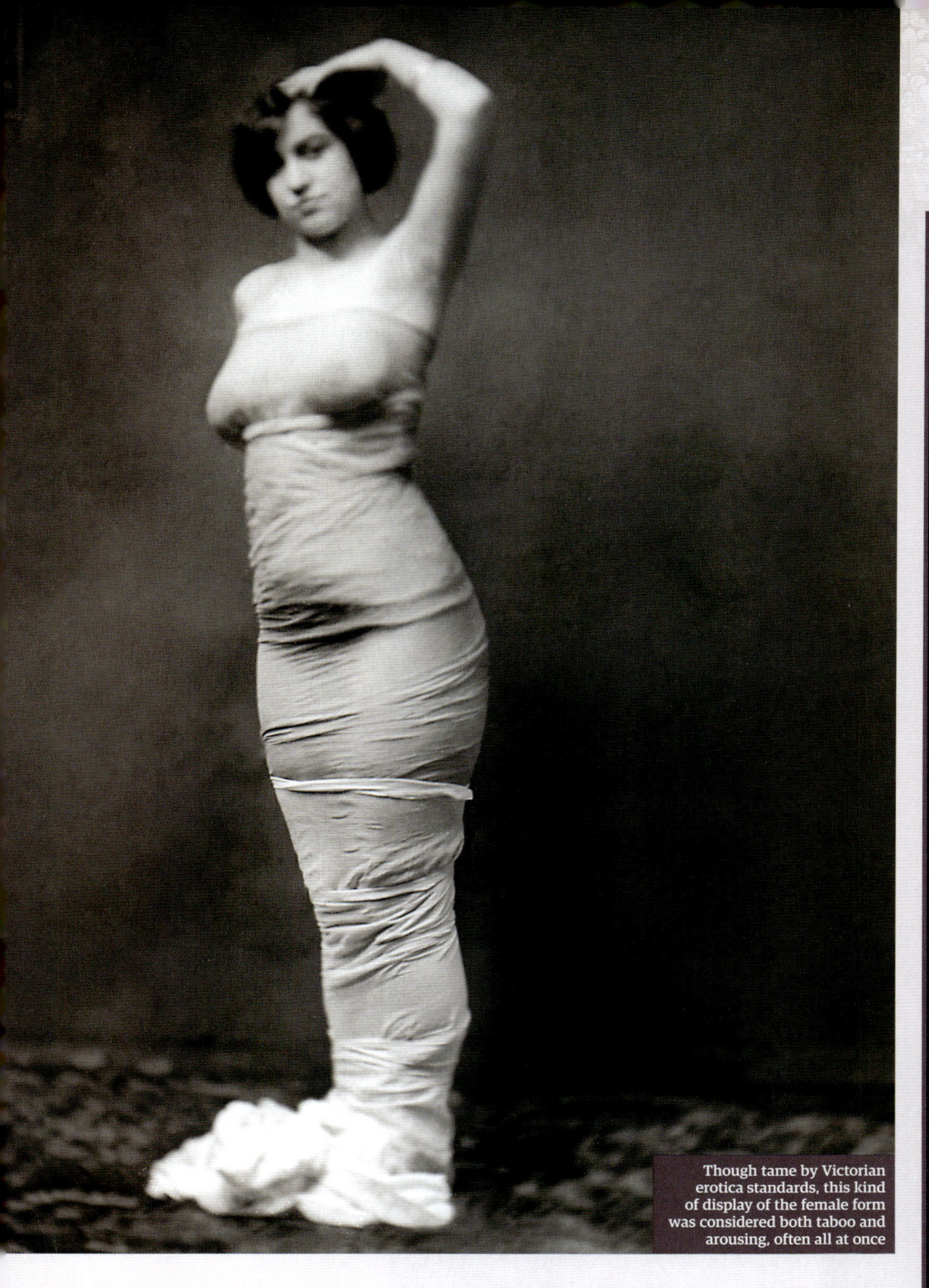

Though tame by Victorian erotica standards, this kind of display of the female form was considered both taboo and arousing, often all at once

THE MALE GAZE

The male gaze dominated much of Victorian society, creating an image of women as either as the ideal or the exact opposite, becoming a threat to order and normality. In polite society, women were pigeonholed as a specifically feminine archetype, with fashions designed to accentuate the figure whilst at the same time suggesting a certain physical restriction.

In entertainment, however, whilst heroines were mostly expected to fit into these stereotypes, women of different thoughts were celebrated. Under the guise of art, literature and theatrical entertainment, women could be explicitly shown as sexual or desirable beings without actual explicit material. Sexually awakened and confident, they posed a tempting threat to men, who it was suggested were unable to resist their machinations. Submitting to them could lead to ruin, as the male gaze was indulged whilst being given the get-out clause of a morality play ending.

THE ERA OF SEX

Victorian sexuality was a place where double standards ran rife. Buttoned up and repressed in public, in private the reality was very different. Attitudes were very different to those of the era's Georgian predecessors and the recovery from this repression would be slow and, ultimately, limited. Today we may joke about the Victorians' prudish attitudes to sex and sexuality, but some are still evident in the modern world we live in today. We may not cover our table legs, but then, neither did the Victorians.

THE QUEEN'S WEDDING NIGHT

Victoria wasn't shy about celebrating the consummation of her marriage

Far from being not amused, Queen Victoria found much to enjoy in her wedding night with Prince Albert on 10 February 1840. Though the public image of the queen is one of a dour, unsmiling woman, when she wed her true love, the truth couldn't have been more different.

In her diaries, she wrote of her adoration of Albert and on the night of their marriage, revelled in "his excessive love and affection", as "he clasped me in his arms, and we kissed each other again and again! Oh! This was the happiest day of my life!" Blissfully in love, she poured out her heart to her diaries, describing the delight as "We both went to bed; to lie by his side and in his arms, and on his dear bosom, and be called by names of tenderness, I have never heard used to me before — was bliss beyond belief!"

Though the young queen's diaries are far from explicit by modern standards, they are an extraordinarily revealing look into her private life, such as we would rarely be privileged to see. Famously, she never truly recovered from Albert's death 21 years later, but in these recollections of their early love, she truly comes alive.

Queen Victoria and Prince Albert enjoyed a passionate and extremely loving marriage, which the queen memorialised in her private diaries

Religion & Belief

62

Contents

Religion & Belief

64 High church, low church
68 Muscular Christianity
70 Superstitions, omens and hauntings
76 Spring-Heeled Jack
78 Victorian occult
88 The Devil's Footprints
90 The Occult Revival
96 Model villages and temperance towns

63

Religion & Belief

High Church Low Church

Victorian churchmanship came in two main forms: smells and bells, or plain and simple

Written by Edoardo Albert

This 1852 painting by Adolph Tidemand perfectly captures the serious and sober sensibility of the Low Church tradition within the Church of England

High Church, Low Church

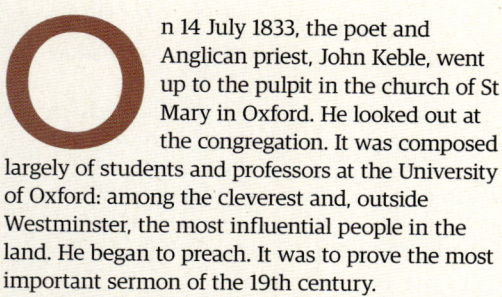

All Saints, Cheltenham, which was built between 1865 and 1868, perfectly reflects the Gothic grandeur of High Church Anglicanism

On 14 July 1833, the poet and Anglican priest, John Keble, went up to the pulpit in the church of St Mary in Oxford. He looked out at the congregation. It was composed largely of students and professors at the University of Oxford: among the cleverest and, outside Westminster, the most influential people in the land. He began to preach. It was to prove the most important sermon of the 19th century.

Keble took as his theme national apostasy. He argued that, contrary to the comfortable imagining of the Church of England, the country as a whole was slipping towards apostasy, a wholesale forgetting of the Christian religion upon which England was based.

This might come as a surprise to us today. We think back on the Victorian era as a time of religious fervour when everyone went to church, very different from today. But that was not the case when John Keble stood up to preach.

The end of the 18th century and the beginning of the 19th century saw the start and development of the Industrial Revolution. Huge numbers of people left the countryside and crowded into new towns and cities, living in close-packed slums. Driven by the changing demands of industry, the population map of the country shifted completely. From most people living spread out in small towns and villages, great swathes of England saw people concentrated into dense cities in houses thrown up as cheaply as possible and then rented out.

But up until the middle of the 19th century, it required an Act of Parliament for the Church of England to build a new church. This meant that vast numbers of people had no access whatsoever to church or any form of Christian teaching.

It was against this backdrop that John Keble stood up to preach. His sermon was all the more striking because Keble had earlier written a book of poems, *The Christian Year*, that would prove the most popular in the Victorian era. He was the gentle prophet of Victorian England.

His sermon had a seismic effect. Among those catalysed by his words were John Henry Newman, Edward Pusey and Augustus Pugin. They, and a group of like-minded individuals, started to produce a series of pamphlets, or tracts, that they called *Tracts for our Times*. This Tractarian Movement argued that the Anglican Church was a branch of the original apostolic church, along with the Catholic and Orthodox churches. As such, the Oxford Movement, as it came to be called, advocated for a renewal of liturgical practices that dated from the first centuries of the church, including the use of incense, a sacramental focus on the Eucharist, and the establishment of religious orders of monks and nuns.

The Tractarians were also intensely aware of the religious deserts in England's industrial towns, and they pioneered new churches in these towns to bring Christianity to the new urban

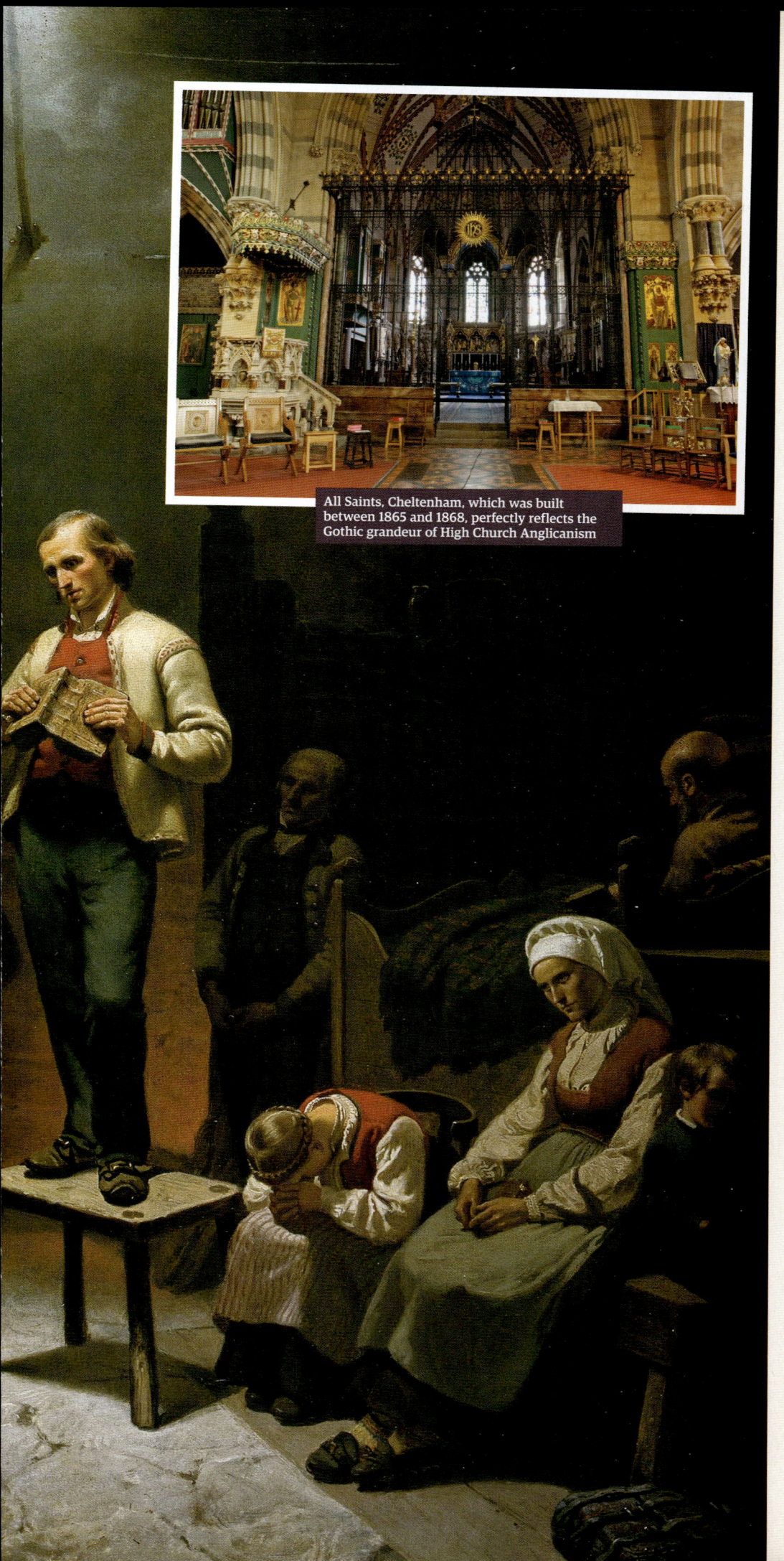

65

Religion & Belief

poor. But they also emphasised beauty, sharing values and aesthetics with the parallel Arts and Crafts Movement.

The architect Augustus Pugin was a leading light of this synthesis. As the man most responsible for the spread of Victorian Gothic architecture, he not only designed the new Houses of Parliament after the old Palace of Westminster burned down in 1834, but he also designed many of the churches that went up in the new towns and the suburbs built in response to the spread of the railways.

The Oxford Movement was the key catalyst for a renewal of High Church Anglicanism, with its emphasis on ritual, ritual beauty and grounding in church history. But it was not the only movement for renewal within the Church of England. At the other pole of religious sensibility, there was also a great growth in Low Church worship. Here, the emphasis was put upon an individual, direct relationship with God, the reading of the Bible and each person's moral efforts.

A seldom-acknowledged root of religious difference is the variation in taste between different people. For its opponents, High Church worship was all smells and bells, vicars wearing richly embroidered vestments and churches intricately decorated on the inside and carved into Victorian Gothic on the outside. Low Church worshippers viewed all of this with suspicion. Their churches were plain, their worship plainer. Indeed, some Low Churchmen implicitly regarded beauty in any form as a snare of the Devil and something to be avoided.

For them, beauty was moral. At their best, they were great social reformers. The Clapham Sect, which included men such as William Wilberforce and Henry Thornton, was crucial to the Abolitionist Movement: its greatest achievement was the ending of the slave trade in 1807 within the British Empire and then the abolition of slavery in 1833, an abolition that the British Empire enforced through its Navy interdicting slave ships of any nation on the high seas.

The contrast and conflict between High and Low Church within the Church of England goes back to the Reformation itself. Henry VIII broke with Rome in 1534, declaring himself rather than the Pope the head of the church in England. But at that point it was by no means clear that the church *in* England would become the Church *of* England. The terms of the Tudor religious settlement were thrashed out during the reigns of Henry VIII and his children; it was the long reign of Elizabeth I which established that England would no longer be a Catholic nation.

What was not settled, however, was what sort of Protestant country England would become. There were essentially two competing visions of Protestantism for England: one had a hierarchical church with bishops and priests and parishes, similar in structure to old Catholic England but ruled by the state rather than the Vatican; the other wanted an England of individual believers united in congregations but with minimal religious hierarchy. The conflict between the two visions became so acute that it provoked the English Civil War. We tend to view the Civil War as a battle for political power between King Charles I and Parliament, but the conflict was underpinned by the religious divisions between the two sides. The Parliamentarians were Puritans, the Royalists wanted to retain the old religious structures and ways of worship.

In the end, the Parliamentarians won the political conflict, but they eventually lost the religious conflict. Puritans, it turns out, are necessary to correct abuses of power but when put in power themselves, as they were during the Commonwealth, they invariably make everyone else so miserable that, following the

The most important figure within the Oxford Movement was John Henry Newman. When he converted to Catholicism in 1845 he took with him much of the movement's intellectual weight

> "SOME LOW CHURCHMEN IMPLICITLY REGARDED BEAUTY IN ANY FORM AS A SNARE OF THE DEVIL"

Restoration of the Monarchy, their ordinances against common festivals were immediately revoked (yes, Parliament did ban Christmas, Easter and Whitsun). England went back to a more hierarchical church, with bishops and vicars.

But another effect of the Civil War was to create a general suspicion of all religious enthusiasm. This suspicion lasted throughout the 18th century. The general view was that religion had its place, particularly in maintaining the legitimacy of the state, but it didn't do to get too carried away with things. After all, it was getting carried away with things that had led to civil war. The 18th century, the century of reason, had no time for such notions.

This meant that by the start of the 19th century, the Church of England was ruled by

High Church, Low Church

PUNCH, OR THE LONDON CHARIVARI.—December 18, 1869.

SLIDING ON THIN ICE.

In 1829 the Catholic Emancipation Act, allowing freedom of worship to Catholics in Britain, was passed in the face of much opposition, so the High Church adoption of practices that were seen as Catholic met much hostility

The Augustus Pugin designed St Cuthbert's Chapel at Ushaw College in Durham illustrates the splendour of Victorian Gothic, which was inspired by the Oxford Movement

Latitudinarians, or the Broad Church as they were also called. This was the party that wanted, essentially, not to rock the boat. The Church was established as an essential part of the ruling elite in England – its bishops sat in the House of Lords, after all. Getting carried away about points of doctrine threatened to ruin all that. What matter if thousands of the poor had no access to Christian teaching? These weren't really the sort of people you wanted in church anyway.

Both the High Church and Low Church movements were reactions against this mildly contemptuous tolerance, although they reacted in different directions.

Although High Church and Low Church were set against each other, their true foes were the people who simply weren't that bothered. Both High Church and Low Church did care, and cared deeply, about the future of the Church of England, although their visions of that church were radically different. Through the energies unleashed by their competition, they re-evangelised England during the latter half of the 19th century, turning the country once again into a self-consciously Christian nation. It was an extraordinary achievement and one that both the High Church and Low Church wings of the Church of England were equally responsible for.

THE SECT THAT ENDED SLAVERY
How a small corner of London revolutionised morals and politics

Every society that we know of practised slavery. As a practice and institution, slavery was even more ubiquitous than marriage. That we now think of slavery as abhorrent rather than simply a normal part of life is, in large part, due to a group of Christian men and women who lived around Clapham, at that time a village south of London, and who worshipped at Holy Trinity Church on Clapham Common. The church still stands there today, its interior and exterior a testament to the plain and simple tastes of the Low Church Clapham Sect. Among the parishioners were William Wilberforce and Henry Thornton, two of the key figures in the campaign against the slave trade. As members of Parliament, Wilberforce and Thornton were instrumental in the passage of the Slave Trade Act in 1807, which banned slavery within the British Empire, and in 1833 the Slavery Abolition Act. The 20th century reacted against Victorian morality, seeing it as prudish and puritanical, but this is to forget what these moralists accomplished, starting with the abolition of slavery and moving on to huge improvements in the living conditions of the new working classes in England. Few others have done so much good and caused so little harm.

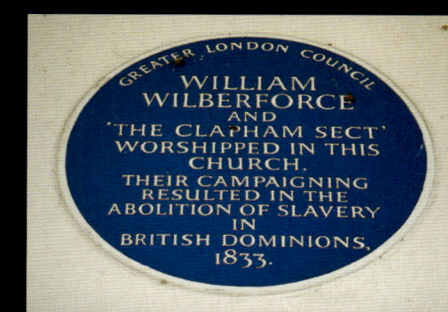

On 26 July 1833, the dying William Wilberforce learned that the bill banning slavery completely from the dominions of the Empire was sure to pass. His life work complete, he died three days later

67

Religion & Belief

MUSCULAR CHRISTIANITY

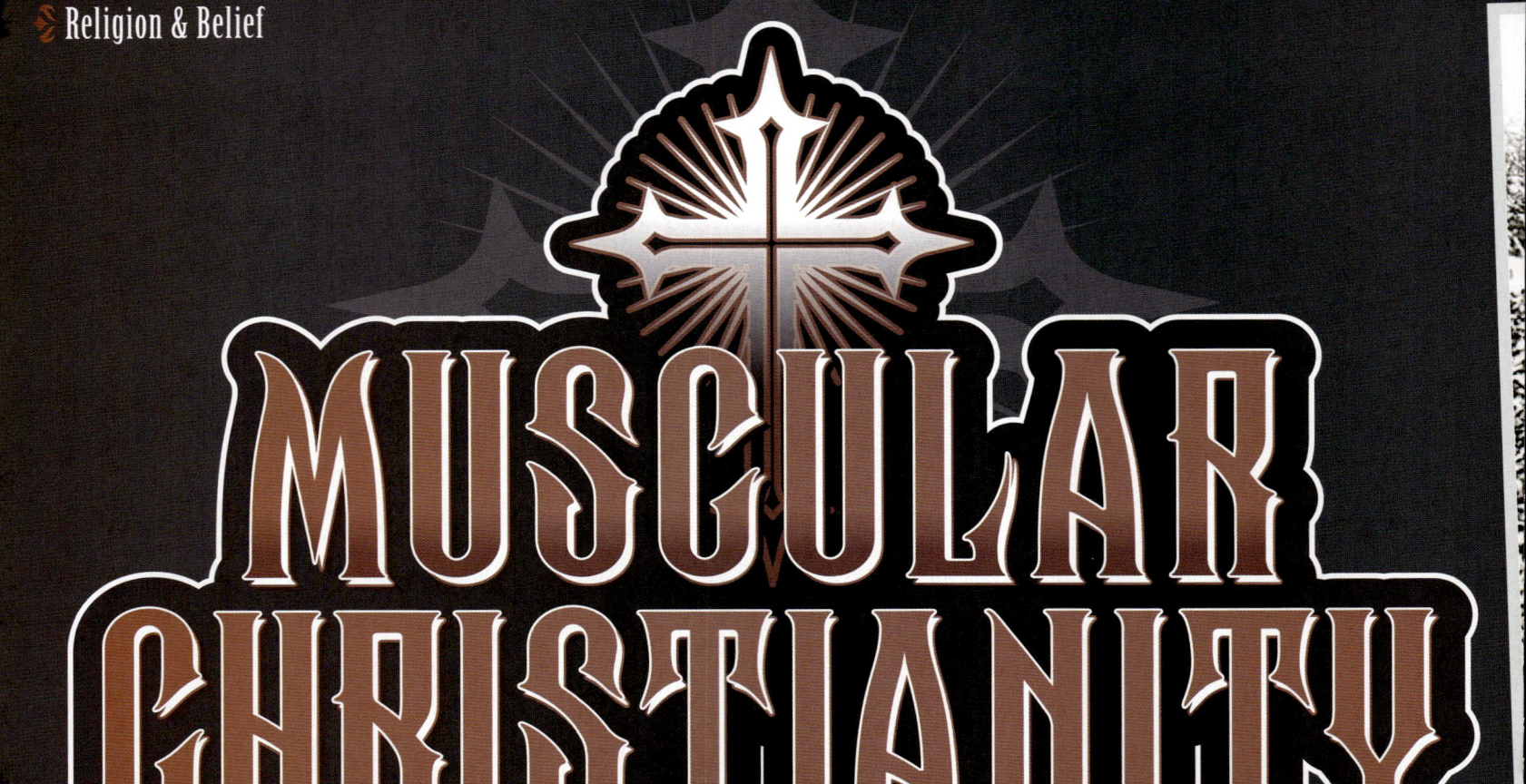

The bond between Christianity and sport and exercise tightened in the mid-19th century with a focus on developing strong and healthy bodies

Written by Jack Griffiths

From the 1850s, a new importance was given to sport and masculinity in Christianity. Known as Muscular Christianity, it centred on the relationship between faith and the ideals of exercise, discipline and masculinity.

The movement began in Britain and then spread elsewhere, particularly to the USA and France. Its genesis began with the works of authors Charles Kingsley and Thomas Hughes. Both men wrote about the robust relationship between patriotism and empire and a strong and athletic population, both through history and in the modern day. Kingsley himself was an advocate for improved adult education and hygiene in the fast-growing dirty cities of Victorian Britain. He believed that Muscular Christianity improved physical and moral health, while Hughes saw it partially as a call-back to the codes of chivalry. Hughes firmly believed in the importance of athletics in Christian ethics, which had been instilled in him from his education at Rugby School.

Muscular Christianity may have grown in popularity partly as a response to the increase in more sedentary jobs as part of industrialisation. It was thought that men needed to express their Christian values with a renewed focus more on sports, exercise and competition, from school-age onwards, to develop their bodies and minds. The focus of the movement was partly to build character and fitness but also to boost flagging numbers of churchgoers and as potential preparation for battle, with Britain still a major global imperial power.

The growth of Muscular Christianity saw the founding of the first Young Men's Christian Association (YMCA) in London in 1844. YMCAs were established as areas in which men could gather for individual and team sports, as well as bonding, with Christian ideals and sportsmanship. The ideas of Muscular Christianity and the YMCA spread to colleges and universities and helped influence ideals that originated at the tail-end of the Victorian era including bodybuilding, the Scout Movement and the rebirth of the Olympics. Pierre de Coubertin, the co-founder of the modern Olympic Games, was an admirer of Hughes' writings and took the ideas of body conditioning and strength into this renaissance of the famous ancient Greek event.

As the role of organised sports began to increase in the Victorian world, it began to separate from the church. As a result, Muscular Christianity faded away but it sowed the seeds for the growth of friendly organised competition and the increased understanding of the importance of exercise to health.

"THE IDEAS OF MUSCULAR CHRISTIANITY HELPED INFLUENCE BODYBUILDING, THE SCOUT MOVEMENT AND THE OLYMPICS"

Muscular Christianity

The first modern Olympic Games was held in Athens in 1896 and some of its origins arose from ideas put forward in Muscular Christianity

Muscular Christianity was embraced by both Catholics and Protestants and was a precursor to the first YMCAs, as well as the Scouts

US President Theodore Roosevelt was a keen believer in Muscular Christianity and his belief further encouraged his fondness for American Football

Religion & Belief

Superstitions Omens and Hauntings

The Victorians have a reputation for hard-nosed rationalism but also put faith in rituals, folklore, and the spirit realm

Written by Ben Gazur

In the popular imagination the Victorians were a pragmatic, industrious, and slightly puritanical people. They had little time for fun and frivolity as they set about laying railway tracks, and building gigantic factories. But that is just one side of the Victorian era and defined mainly by the men (and one woman) at the top who ran the British Empire. For the majority of people life was very little like the stereotype. The Victorian period was one where superstitions, folklore, and spirits still held sway.

It is possible to track how the elite viewed such matters through newspapers and books of the time. Many folk traditions were referred to as mere delusions held by the uneducated masses, while the elite were too clever to believe in such things as ghosts or omens. Part of the reason this narrative was pushed was to reinforce the idea that the lower classes were not capable of thinking for themselves and therefore could not take part in the democratic running of the nation.

Most people however clung to the superstitions of which they had been taught because it brought order to their lives. A woman who was forced to bake bread all day knew that cutting a cross in the top of her loaves would keep the Devil out of them and ensure they rose well in the oven. The man on his way to work in the mines might take comfort from various good luck signs, like seeing a chimney sweep, before he descended into the dark and dangerous pit he dug.

Though many educated people might have disdained superstitions and tales of ghosts, an academic interest in such beliefs did arise. It is thanks to Victorian scholars of folklore that many of these traditions were recorded and studied which otherwise might have disappeared forever. The rational elite may have laughed at superstitions, but they were also fascinated by them.

What's more, the decline in literal belief in the Bible during the Victorian period created a gap in the popular imagination which could be filled by new types of spirituality. Spiritualist mediums claimed to be able to communicate with the dead and their popularity increased towards the last years of the 19th century. Soon seances were occurring in the parlours of even the most aristocratic families. Somehow the ghosts which had once been mocked were now being talked to and studied.

Here are some of the most popular, and oddest, folkloric aspects of the Victorians...

> "THE DECLINE IN LITERAL BELIEF IN THE BIBLE DURING THE VICTORIAN PERIOD CREATED A GAP IN THE POPULAR IMAGINATION WHICH COULD BE FILLED BY NEW TYPES OF SPIRITUALITY"

Superstitions, Omens and Hauntings

The Victorians loved fiction featuring ghosts, like *A Christmas Carol*, but many really believed in the supernatural

Religion & Belief

MARRIAGE OMENS AND LORE

Marrying well was all important for a Victorian woman, a good husband meant a happy life while a bad one could ruin it. So to predict whether they would be lucky in love they sought out a number of omens on their wedding day. Certain animals crossing the bride's path, like a pig, were dreadful bad luck. Meeting a funeral procession on your way to the church signified nothing good. Sunshine, of course, predicted a glorious future for the couple.

Certain days of the week were thought of as predicting the outcome of the marriage, with some days to be avoided at all costs. A popular rhyme ran:

*"Monday for wealth,
Tuesday for health,
Wednesday the best of all.
Thursday for crosses,
Friday for losses,
Saturday no luck at all."*

For extra luck the bride could place a silver sixpence in her left shoe to show that she would be walking into good fortune.

The tradition of a bride wearing white on her wedding day began with the marriage of Queen Victoria in 1840

A Victorian baby stood around a 15 per cent chance of death in their first year, so anything to preserve their health was tried

LUCKY BABIES

In times when mortality rates for infants were high, like the Victorian era, parents turned to superstitions to protect them. When a baby was born they thought that pressing a silver coin into its hand would bring it good fortune, but there were regional variations. In the north of England a baby would be presented with an egg and some salt by neighbours – and if they forgot to bring the gifts then the parents would often complain. This egg was not eaten but pierced and the contents blown out. The name of the egg-giver was then inked onto the shell and as long as the eggshell was preserved the baby would enjoy good health.

If they wanted their child to grow up to be wealthy then some parents wrapped up an infant's right hand to signify that they would learn to hold on to money.

Superstitions, Omens and Hauntings

GHOSTLY HOMES AND HOUSES

Victorian literature was steeped in Gothic imagery and ghost stories were some of the most popular tales written at the time. But there was also a burgeoning genre of books containing collections of hauntings that were believed to be true.

In *The Night-Side of Nature: or Ghosts and Ghost-Seers*, published in 1850, Catherine Crowe reported many ghost sightings across Britain. She told of ghostly footsteps in the night which haunted anyone who stayed in a certain room in a grand old house. In another home, a man complained of apparitions peeping through his bed curtains all night, and he fled the next day. Ghosts seemed to like annoying the sleepy. One man's bedclothes were repeatedly snatched away and flung across the room in the night.

Some of the ghosts became famous. Many noble families laid claim to ghosts like 'Spinning Jenney' whose spinning wheel could be heard whirring in the night. Others pointed to Grey Ladies who wandered their corridors.

Many viewed such tales as mere superstition but the rise of Spiritualism gave educated people a quasi-scientific method to investigate ghosts and other supernatural phenomena. The invention of photography and the many ghostly images captured seemed to provide proof that there really were spectres out there.

A photo of the library in Combermere Abbery, taken in 1891, was studied by Arthur Conan Doyle as proof of ghosts

DIVINATION OF DREAMS

A number of guides to the interpretation of dreams were published in the Victorian era, and they reveal a great deal about what people were concerned about at the time. Dreaming of sitting on the seashore, for instance, meant that you would soon travel to a distant part of the globe – as many were during the heyday of the empire. Check what you were sitting on in the dream however, as sitting on rock meant a safe and pleasant trip, but sitting on grass foretold a shipwreck.

Some portents in dreams were the opposite of what one might expect. Dreaming of a ring meant that you would soon break up with someone you were attached to, while dreaming of sickness meant a wedding – though perhaps not a happy one. It was bad luck if you dreamed of reading in a library as it predicted you would never marry and have to find contentment in books. For men dreaming of a queen meant he would be ruled by his wife to such an extent that "without her permission he will not get so much as a lump of sugar."

Tales of people who were saved from disasters by prophetic dreams were eagerly read by an audience who believed in the power of dreams.

The was much debate in the Victorian era over whether prophetic dreams might be sent by divine sources or some natural human psychic ability

Religion & Belief

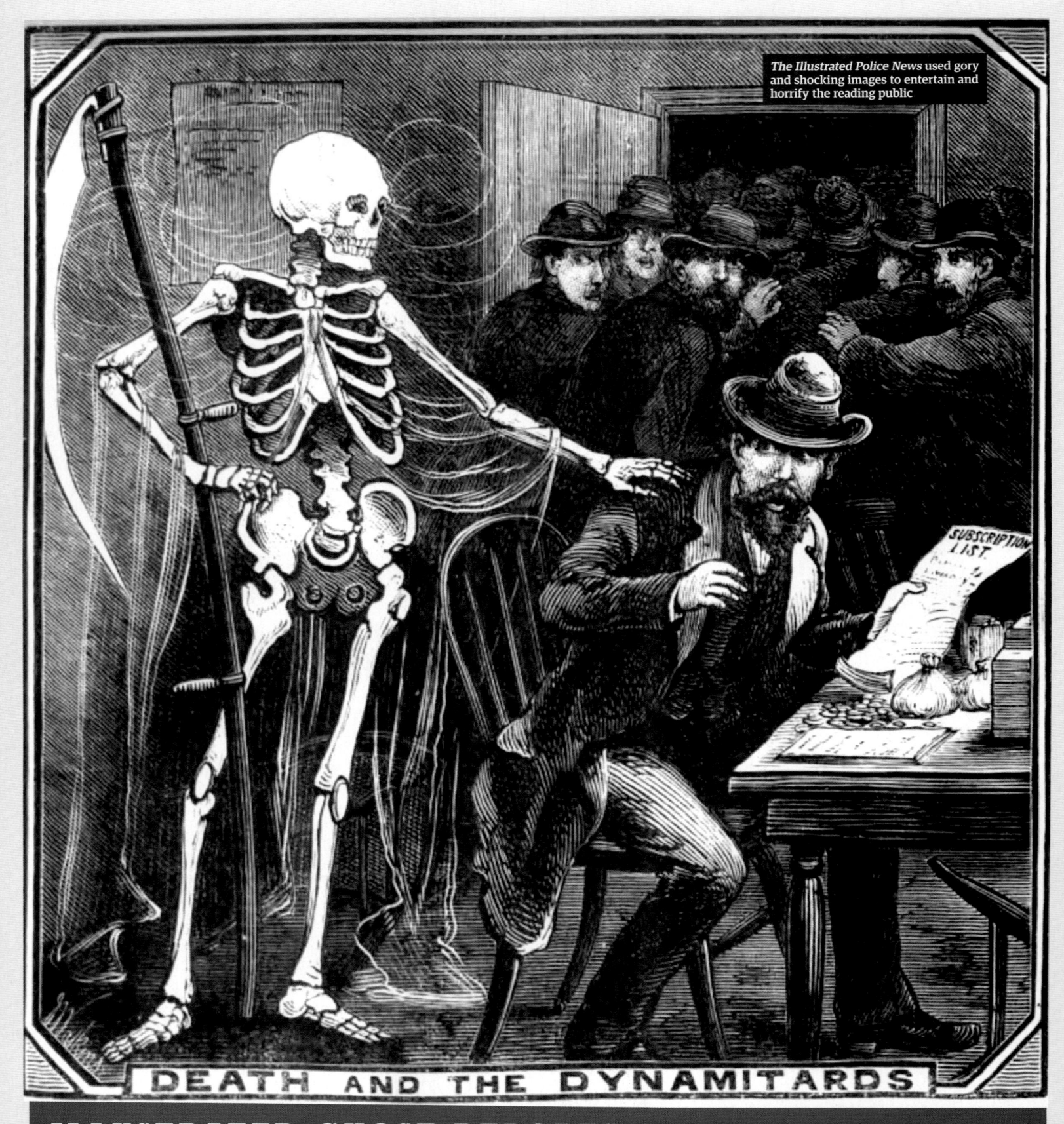

The Illustrated Police News used gory and shocking images to entertain and horrify the reading public

DEATH AND THE DYNAMITARDS

ILLUSTRATED GHOST REPORTS

The Illustrated Police News was a weekly Victorian paper reporting on crimes and other events, often alongside lurid drawings. In 1898 they printed the story of a headless ghost alarming the people of Buckingham.

One farmer reported that it appeared to him as a headless woman in a long shroud which caused his horse to back into a ditch. When the ghost continued to harass the farmer he begged her 'in the name of God' to speak instead of simply hanging there. She then drifted away through a dense hedge. Whether the police ever apprehended this menacing ghost was unfortunately never recorded.

Superstitions, Omens and Hauntings

VICTORIAN FUNERAL BLUES

British cities are dotted with Victorian graveyards with elaborate mausoleums. Burying the dead was a serious business and had to be done right. The moment a person stopped breathing the clocks in the house were stopped to mark the time and prevent chiming disturbing their spirit. The mirrors were draped with black cloth to stop their soul getting lodged in the reflection. When the time came for the funeral the body had to be carried out feet first otherwise their spirit might look back into the home and be drawn back to haunt it – or call out for another member of the family to join them in death.

Victorian funerals were surrounded by traditions and superstitions designed to ease the spirit of the deceased

WILD FEATHERS, HARD DEATH

The Victorians notoriously loved a melancholy death scene in their literature but in real life people sought to make their loved one's departure from this life as easy as possible. Having the feathers of a wild bird, such as pigeons or waterfowl, in the mattress that an ill person slept on was believed to keep them clinging to life. So, to ease their passing, the sick were moved to a bed made from chicken or goose feathers, or simply lain on the floor. Should you wish to prolong their life so that they could receive an important guest then a wild feather could be placed in their pillow.

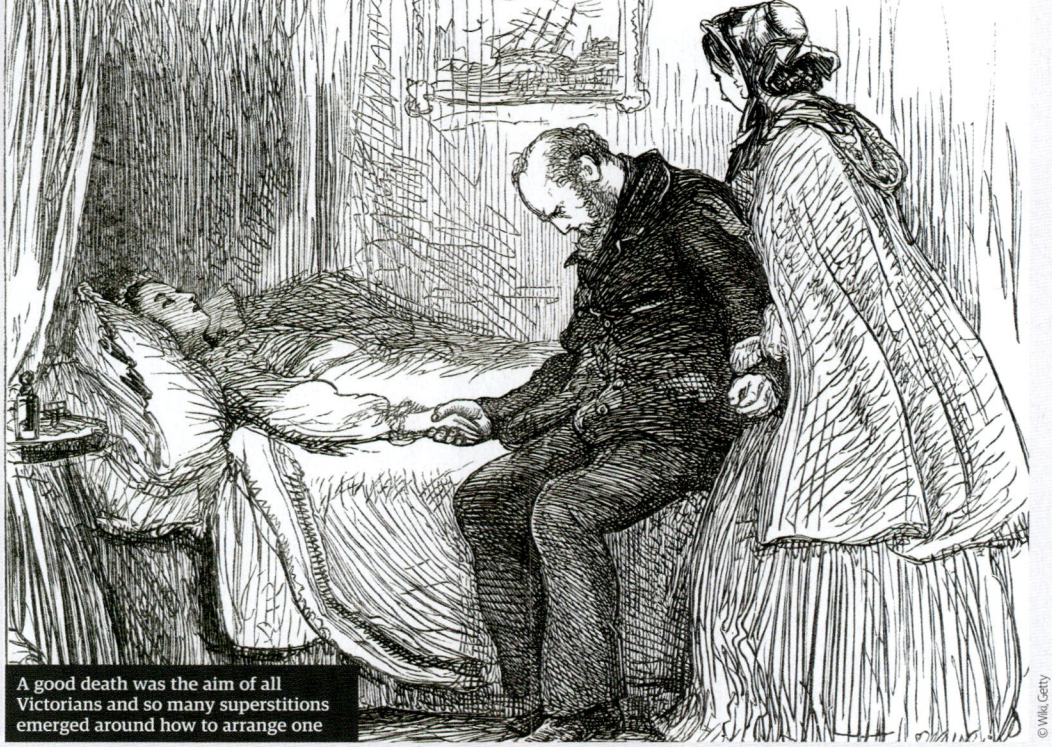

A good death was the aim of all Victorians and so many superstitions emerged around how to arrange one

Religion & Belief

Spring Heeled Jack

Victorian England was completely enthralled by reports of a terrifying supernatural creature that attacked young women on the streets of London

Written by Melanie Clegg

At a time when the British public was fascinated by gothic novels, penny dreadfuls, spooky theatricals and séances, it's hardly surprising that rumours of ghosts and other malign spirits stalked the nation's streets in search of unwary citizens to terrorise. The first known sighting of Spring Heeled Jack, who would become the most famous manifestation of this, occurred in October 1837 when a young woman reported being violently attacked by a peculiar, clawed assailant while walking across Clapham Common. Her screams frightened him off, but the following evening, he struck again, leaping out at a carriage in order to force it off the road before, as witnesses would later claim, jumping over a 9ft wall to make his escape.

Over the following months, tales about the so-called Spring Heeled Jack proliferated as a number of young women in London claimed to have been attacked by a demonic creature with a corpse-like face, sharp claws, fiery red eyes and the extraordinary ability to leap over high walls. The panic became even more intense in February 1838 when two teenage girls were attacked, with both reporting that their terrifying assailant "presented a most hideous and frightful appearance" and spurted blue and white flames from his mouth.

The newspapers were filled with stories and theories about the mysterious Jack, while the public avidly read numerous pamphlets and penny dreadfuls about his exploits. Although many people enjoyed attributing the attacks to a malevolent supernatural being, others believed that marauding young noblemen were to blame, with the young Marquess of Waterford, who was known to love pranks and never turn down a wager, being the number one suspect.

There were several alleged sightings of Spring Heeled Jack over the rest of the century, although they dwindled away and became increasingly rare by the end of the 1840s. In 1877, a soldier on sentry duty at Aldershot Barracks reported being accosted by a peculiar figure who slapped his face

Spring Heeled Jack

One of the earliest alleged attacks by Spring Heeled Jack involved him jumping out at a carriage and forcing it off the road

Spring Heeled Jack's exploits fascinated the nation, spawning dozens of penny dreadfuls detailing sightings, both real and imaginary

Although accounts of Jack's appearance varied, all of his alleged victims agreed that his ability to leap over walls in one bound was definitely supernatural

and then leapt away "with astonishing bounds" when fired at, while in 1888 he allegedly made an appearance on a church roof in Liverpool before bounding away into the night. Although by now most people believed sightings to be nothing more sinister than the work of pranksters, there is no doubt that Spring Heeled Jack was an integral and significant part of Victorian culture, with even the most sceptical readers reading about his exploits. Soon parents scared their children into good behaviour by threatening them with a visit from Spring Heeled Jack if they didn't behave themselves, the devilish trickster turned folk hero and useful bogeyman.

> "A NUMBER OF YOUNG WOMEN CLAIMED TO HAVE BEEN ATTACKED BY A DEMONIC CREATURE WITH THE EXTRAORDINARY ABILITY TO LEAP OVER HIGH WALLS"

Religion & Belief

VICTORIAN OCCULT

Lifting the shroud on the 19th century's obsession with death and the afterlife

Written by Callum McKelvie

On 1 April 1848, ten-year-old Catherine Fox and her sister Margaret, 14, received a mysterious visitor at their home in New York – a ghost. The spirit, which went by the name Mr Splitfoot (a popular name for the devil at the time) communicated with the girls through a series of 'rappings' – tapping out messages on a hard surface. It was able to discern their ages and answer questions they put to it. Later, the phantom claimed to be the ghost of peddler Charles B Rosna who, five years earlier, had been murdered and buried in the cellar.

As a result of these strange events, the girls and their supposed powers caught the public's attention. They first visited Rochester and demonstrated their 'rapping' for a paying audience, later making regular appearances in New York City. Having performed for such personalities as historian George Bancroft and novelist James Fenimore Cooper, the girls became a popular entertainment act and news of their otherworldly abilities spread to Great Britain. Of course, no one took any notice that the day the Fox sisters first 'communed' with Mr Splitfoot also happened to be April Fool's Day.

"The Fox sisters created the first craze for spiritualism," says Simone Natale, author of *Supernatural Entertainments: Victorian Spiritualism And The Rise Of Mass Media Culture*. "What I find interesting is that the emergence of spiritualism is considered to begin in the small town of Huddersfield in the state of New York, where they first reported experiencing this phenomena. However, really their demonstration in Rochester should be considered the beginning. This was the first time spiritualism was presented as a sensation to a paying public. The Fox sisters also had managers and people who handled their relationship with the press, so there was an element of show business."

Soon other mediums appeared, demonstrating their abilities in return for money. In the US and Europe, a spiritualism craze began as mesmerism, mediumship and magic fuelled the public imagination, seemingly in contradiction to the simultaneous growth in rational and scientific thought. The Victorian relationship with the supernatural is an interesting one in the supposed age of scientific reasoning, the era of Darwin

Victorian Occult

Religion & Belief

and the century of Chambers. Yet the Victorian obsession with death and any possibility of life afterwards cannot be denied. Due to the Fox sisters' hoax, a bizarre mix of sensationalist sideshowery and serious scientific investigation began and lasted until the end of the century and into the next, in the United States, Britain and most of Europe.

One of the initial starting points for spiritualism's spread into the United Kingdom was a visit by the medium Maria B Hayden. Setting sail with her husband in October of 1852, their arrival was met she was aware of facts whose details he had revealed to no one. Charging a guinea for her services, her husband also launched a publication on the topic of mediums and spiritualism entitled *The Spirit World* (that only lasted one issue). Whether sceptics or believers, there was no denying people's interest in Hayden and soon table tapping developed into a popular pastime.

However, not all proved as successful as Hayden. Throughout the century there were scandals involving many popular mediums that exposed their various 'tricks of the trade' and ended their careers.

> "During a seance in 1855 a particularly embarrassing scene occurred when he presented an apparition to the poet Robert Browning and proclaimed it to be the latter's son who had died in infancy"

with some controversy and there were many who disputed their claims. Despite this, the Haydens attracted the attention of numerous upper class personalities, including Charles Young (described as the leading tragedian actor of his time), Sir Charles Isham and royal physician Dr John Ashburner. They publicly expressed their amazement at Maria Hayden's supernatural abilities, with Young in particular struggling to understand how

Perhaps one of the most notorious of these swindlers was Daniel Donglas Home, who was involved in several scandals. During a seance in 1855 a particularly embarrassing scene occurred when he presented an apparition to the poet Robert Browning and proclaimed it to be the latter's son who had died in infancy. The apparition was unveiled to be Home's bare foot, made all the more awkward because Browning had had no such child.

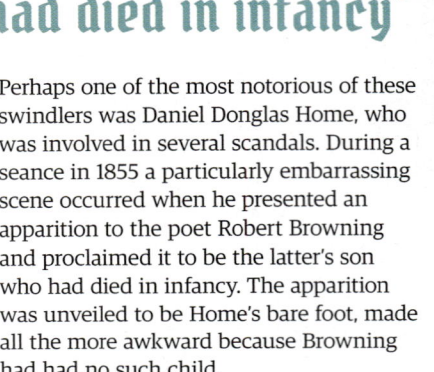

BELOW
An illustration of a seance, c.1887

Browning's encounters and subsequent anger with Home would later inspire his poem *Mr Sludge – 'The Medium'*, which opens with the line: "Now don't, Sir! Don't expose me!" Surprisingly this seems to have been a favourite trick of Home's as barrister Frederick Merrifield also claimed to have witnessed the use of the phantom foot, as well as a fake arm attached to Home's own. Frank Herme and Charles Williams were two other nefarious tricksters who came unstuck. In 1875 the duo were caught out when the latter acted the part of a spirit by clothing himself in two yards of 'stiffened muslin, wound round his head and hanging down as far as his thigh'.

One of the most notorious spirit-scandals, however, avoided mediumship entirely and relied on the use of a relatively new piece of technology – the camera. At some point during the 1860s a young American photographer, William Mumler, was developing one of his pictures and was startled to see the visage of his dead cousin in the image. Discovering a knack for photographing spirits of the dead, the enterprising Mumler was able to turn this into a business opportunity and soon had many clients, including Abraham Lincoln's widow Mary Todd Lincoln.

Victorian Occult

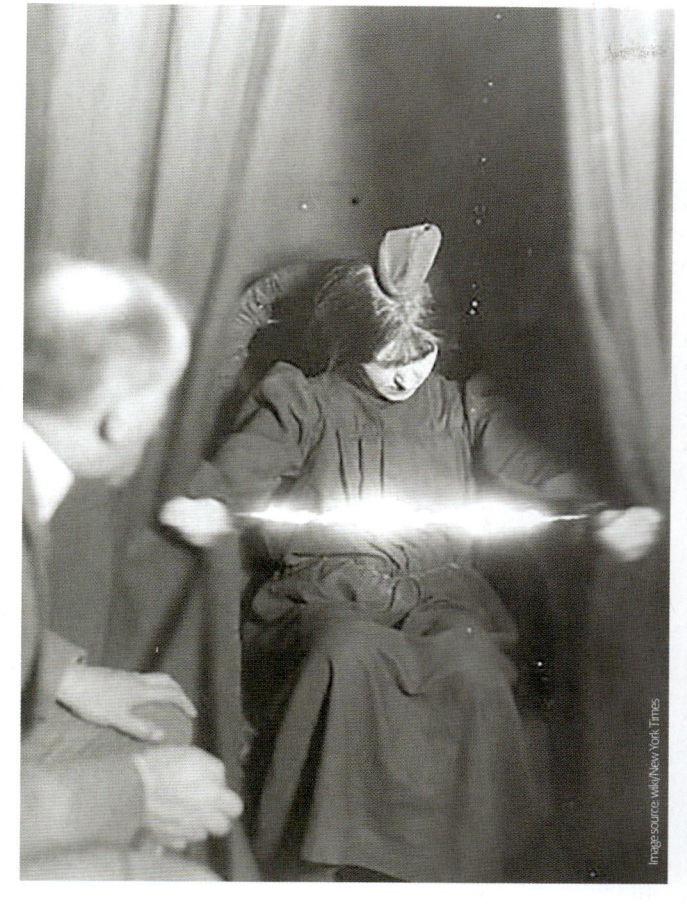

As Mumler's business grew it became increasingly reliant on grieving families whose loved ones had perished in the Civil War. This brought with it a certain amount of fame and notoriety, as Mumler found himself with a long list of enemies committed to exposing him as a fraud.

One of his most vociferous opponents was PT Barnum, the American entrepreneur and businessman. Barnum took particular dislike to Mumler's exploits and claimed, among other allegations, that the photographer had broken into homes in order to obtain pre-existing photographs of clients' loved ones. Mumler was eventually placed on trial for fraud and Barnum testified against him. In one particularly damning piece of evidence, Barnum hired Abraham Bogaerdus to replicate Mumler's effect and create a photograph that showed Barnum with the ghost of Abraham Lincoln. This, along with the gradual realisation that the numerous 'spirits' photographed by Mumler were actually still among the living, left his reputation in tatters. Despite being acquitted and resuming his career as a portrait photographer, he never again dabbled in the spirit world.

However, Mumler had not been alone in his use of 'spirit' photography, nor did belief in the possibility die out following his trial. It remained a popular exploit throughout the century and today a variety of examples can be found in museums across the world.

"The relationship between spiritualism and evidence is a very important element," says Natale. "One of the things that happens with spirit photography is that it provides a form of evidence. Around the same time that spirit photographers were producing their works, there was a lot of doubt within the spiritualist movement that these could be trusted. In fact, there were attempts to get testimonies from people who witnessed spirit photographs being developed. However, in my opinion, the key thing was that photography was part of an emerging visual culture that started in the 1860s. At this time there were the first developments of photography as a mass medium. They were printed, circulated and used as a visual curiosity, a form of entertainment, and the same thing happened with spirit photography. It also presented a material object that was visually compelling and prints were sold by spiritualist publishers or presented in lectures alongside the magic lantern."

Elsewhere in the United States, another spiritual renaissance was occurring. These days New Orleans has a reputation as one of the USA's paranormal hot spots and

ABOVE-LEFT An 1840s illustration for Charles Dickens' *A Christmas Carol*

ABOVE A photo of the fraud Eva Carrière during a seance, with light between her hands

RIGHT From left: Margaret, Catherine and Leah Fox

Religion & Belief

GHOST STORIES

Five mysterious hauntings and supernatural happenings that obsessed 19th century Britain

The Hammersmith Ghost

Towards the end of 1803, several people claimed to have been attacked by a malevolent spirit in the Hammersmith area of London. Believed to be a suicide victim whose soul could not rest as they hadn't been buried in consecrated ground, two female victims died from fright and a brewer's servant was attacked in a graveyard. As a result local men armed themselves and patrolled the streets, among them one Francis Smith. Smith came across bricklayer Thomas Milwood, who was entirely clad in white for his work. Panicking, Smith shot and killed Milwood. The resultant trial set important legal precedents regarding accountability and mistaken belief.

The Electric Horror Of Berkeley Square

A notorious hotspot for supernatural happenings during the latter half of the 19th century, many ghosts walked the halls of 50 Berkeley Square in central London. A particular room on the second floor caused more fear than most, however, and tales include a young maid found screaming, dying shortly afterwards, and Lord Thomas Lyttelton shooting at a mysterious creature in the night. In 1879 an issue of *Mayfair Magazine* reported that "the very party walls of the house, when touched, were found saturated with an electric horror".

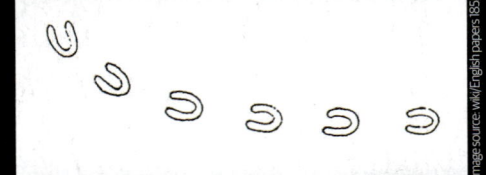

Spring-Heeled Jack

Without a doubt the most famous Victorian legend is that of Spring-Heeled Jack, who terrorised the streets of London between 1837 and 1904. There were numerous sightings, but none more frightening than Jane Alsop's. On the night of 19 February 1838, she opened her door to a man claiming to be a police officer, who requested a candle because they had caught Spring-Heeled Jack in a nearby alley. As soon as she left the house, however, the man threw off his cloak, revealing a strange oilskin helmet, metallic claws and red blazing eyes. Shooting balls of blue fire from his mouth, he attacked Alsop before her sister ran to her aid and he fled. Jack became a common part of Victorian folklore and was extremely popular in the penny dreadfuls of the time.

Devil's Footprints

In February of 1855, trails of strange hoof marks appeared overnight in the snow. Covering a distance of 40 to 100 miles, they appeared on the tops of houses, fields, gardens, and in places enclosed by high walls. Local parishioners feared the marks had been left by Old Nick himself and numerous explanations, including an escaped kangaroo, have been touted ever since.

The Grey Man Of The Theatre Royal

The Theatre Royal on Dury Lane in London plays host to many spectres, the most famous being the Grey Man, an 18th century nobleman. In the late 1870s legend has it that workmen uncovered a bricked-up skeleton with a sword protruding from its ribs. Could this have been the Grey Man himself?

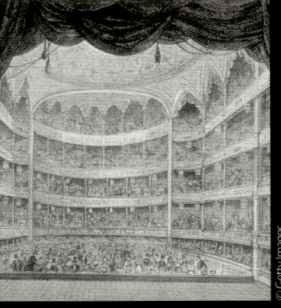

Victorian Occult

ABOVE Contemporary illustration of a voodoo ceremony

RIGHT Mary Todd Lincoln in the photo that was said to show the ghost of Abraham Lincoln

much of this reputation rests on the city's connection to voodoo. 'Louisiana Voodoo' is a form of spiritualism based on the traditional Haitian religion and began in the mid 1700s, flourishing during the 19th century. In this period, no practitioner was more powerful than Marie Laveau, one of 15 'Voodoo Queens'.

Born around 1801 to the former slave Marguerite Henry D'Arcantel and Charles Laveaux, much of her life is shrouded in mystery. Entering into a relationship with

yelling… [in] the hellish observance of the mysterious rites of Voudou… one of the worst forms of African paganism."

In 1874, she held a rite for St John's Eve on the shores of Lake Pontchartrain that attracted some 12,000 followers. Laveau's most integral contribution, however, was in furthering the introduction of elements of Roman Catholicism into traditional voodoo, a practice which had begun during the religion's initial import in the early 18th century.

have been a lifelong obsession. In January 1880 he attended a lecture entitled *Does Death End All?* and wrote to his mother saying it was "very clever thing indeed," but ultimately claimed that it was, "not convincing to me."

Thirteen years later, in 1893, his interest had developed enough to persuade him to join the Society For Psychical Research. His focus was always primarily towards the spiritual and the dead as opposed to areas such as mesmerism, although he was known to occasionally dabble in that too. However, more often than not his time with the society was taken up by experimenting with 'table tapping' and automatic writing. Conan Doyle's fascination with the spiritual would eventually caused it to surface in his stories. His short story *Playing With Fire*, for example, tells of a group of people struggling with the consequences of a seance. Perhaps the most striking example is one of his later novels, *The Land Of Mist* (1926), featuring the hero of *The Lost World*, the hot-tempered Professor Edward Challenger. The story deals directly with spiritualism, even to the extent of having its sceptical hero converted into a believer at the book's conclusion. Somewhat troublingly, the second section of *The Land Of Mist* suggests that the Central Intelligence (God)

> ## "Mumler was developing one of his photos and was startled to see the visage of his dead cousin in the image"

Christophe Glapion, a descendent of an aristocratic French family, they moved into a creole cottage and it was here around 1820 that Laveau began practitioning. She opened a beauty parlour aimed at some of the wealthier families in New Orleans, which not only provided her with the latest gossip but also with a place through which to sell her charms and dolls. In the 1850s her fame as a Voodoo Queen led to several accounts of her activities in local newspapers, with one in particular noting: "Marie and her wenches were continuously disturbing the peace and that of the neighbourhood with their fighting and obscenity and infernal singing and

Back in Great Britain, the spiritualist obsession was in full-swing. The Society For Psychical Research was founded in 1882 with the intention of investigating ("without prejudice or prepossession of any kind") various paranormal phenomena and acted as an extremely fierce proponent of the movement. Several decades earlier in 1862, The Ghost Club had been formed for much the same reason. Originally having its roots in discussions between fellows at Cambridge, it counted Arthur Conan Doyle and Charles Dickens among its members. Often incorrectly assumed to be a result of the death of Conan Doyle's son Kingsley in 1918, Conan Doyle's interest may well

83

Religion & Belief

punished humanity for laughing at the possibility of an afterlife by instigating the slaughter of World War I.

Conan Doyle was by no means the only literary figure of this era to turn to the supernatural as inspiration for his stories. As the public interest in phantoms and spooks grew, it didn't confine itself simply to table tapping and soon seeped into popular culture as well. Penny dreadfuls (cheap, sensationalist novels), theatre productions and gothic melodramas all became obsessed with the spirit world.

More than any other medium however, the 19th and early 20th century was the golden age of the ghost story as writers such as MR James and Charles Dickens created some of the most bloodcurdling tales of terror the world had yet seen. Between them, these two authors would bring something new to the ghost story and help cement the form as a Christmas tradition. James had a yuletide habit of reading his tales to his students at Cambridge, while Dickens published *A Christmas Carol*, perhaps the most famous seasonal ghost tale of all. James's stories did not appear in print until 1904, but came to define the burgeoning ghost tale genre.

Arguably his most celebrated work is *Oh, Whistle And I'll Come To You, My Lad*, which tells the story of an academic's stay at an isolated seaside resort and the events that occur when he discovers a strange whistle on a beach. Often featuring as their protagonists fussy academics who find themselves facing off against supernatural forces, the stories can be seen as narrative battles between the growing reliance on scepticism and rational thought against more traditional superstitions.

James and Dickens were not alone, however, and other famous authors attempted to get in on the act. Robert Louis Stevenson's 1884 story *The Body Snatcher* draws on the Burke and Hare murders of 1828, in which the two had turned to homicide in order to procure fresh corpses for Dr Robert Knox and his medical students. Featuring a rather nasty supernatural twist in the tale, the story is a perfect example of the combination of the Victorian love for the grim and grisly with the paranormal. Towards the end of the century, even Oscar Wilde got in on the act with *The Canterville Ghost* (1887), an amusing pastiche in which the ghost is the one who is haunted.

Among numerous key figures within the spiritualist movement, one of the most interesting was newspaper editor WT Stead. To this day, Stead remains controversial for his article series such as *The Maiden Tribute Of Modern Babylon*, which created a state of moral panic and was instrumental in the creation of the Criminal Law Amendment Act of 1885. As the articles dealt primarily with child prostitution, Stead used unlawful methods of investigative journalism to procure his information and spent three months in prison as a result. Through his radical journalistic style of involving his personal opinions he was able to influence contemporary society and politics.

In the 1890s Stead developed a strong interest in spiritualism and founded the quarterly journal *Borderland* in 1893. Running until 1897, the magazine was

ABOVE-LEFT & RIGHT Author of *Sherlock Holmes* and devoted spiritualist Arthur Conan Doyle

ABOVE Voodoo Queen Marie Laveau

Victorian Occult

> "As the public interest in phantoms and spooks grew, penny dreadfuls, theatre productions and gothic melodramas all became obsessed with the spirit world"

targeted towards the general public as opposed to members of the Society For Psychical Research or other individuals with a vested interest in the topic. Perhaps one of his most inventive decisions was to employ one Ada Goodrich Freer as his assistant editor, who wrote primarily under the pseudonym Miss X.

A medium, clairvoyant and psychical researcher, Freer was member of the Society For Psychical Research and became acquainted with John Crichton-Stuart, the Third Marquess of Bute, a devoted spiritualist who organised several investigations into the topic throughout his lifetime. One of the more famous involved Freer in an attempt to discover the causes of reputed hauntings at Ballechin House, a Georgian estate in Perthshire, Scotland, which had been owned by Major Robert Steuart in the mid-19th century. Steuart had returned to the house in the 1850s after serving in the Indian Army, during which time he'd developed a strong belief in reincarnation as well as a somewhat intense admiration for man's canine companions. On several occasions he was reputed to have said that after he died he would return in the form of a dog.

Following Steuart's death, his young nephew inherited Ballechin House and, obviously fearing the major's four-legged return, promptly executed the all dogs on the estate with a rifle. As a result of this the major, his spirit having been denied its furry body, began haunting the halls of Ballechin. Enter Freer, who stayed in the house between February and April of 1897. During her stay she would regularly read aloud from the *Office Of The Dead* (a prayer cycle for long-dead souls) and strange sounds were recorded. Her findings were then printed and published in *The Alleged Haunting of B-- House*, which stated it's intention as "not for the establishment of theories but for the record of fact". However, public interest in this investigation was highly critical and a June 1897 issue of *The Times* newspaper included a particularly harsh assessment of the events. In particular, Freer was targeted and, rather than standing by one of their own, the Society For Psychical Research quickly disowned the clairvoyant and discredited all findings of the investigation. Freer's relationship with the society never fully recovered and she fled first to Jerusalem and then America before fading into obscurity.

As the decades wore on, interest in the spiritual and supernatural never really went away. It would be easy to assume that the public fascination in spiritualism and the occult faded due to World War I as the mechanised horror of that conflict caused people to doubt their beliefs, but that would not be true. If anything, while popular interest began to wane in the years prior to the war, the conflict caused another boom in interest as people sought to commune with those they had lost. Physicist Oliver Lodge, who had long been a member of The Ghost Club, published *Raymond* in 1916, which told of his communication with his son Raymond,

BELOW Seances and photos depicting 'spirits' were popular with the Victorians

Religion & Belief

who had been killed at Ypres in 1915. The book was incredibly popular and inspired others to attempt to commune with loved ones they'd lost during the war.

Even over successive decades, interest in the spiritual and supernatural never quite went away. In the 1920s and 1930s, interest in occult philosophy overtook more spiritualist leanings and the works of Dennis Wheatley and Aleister Crowley captured the public imagination. Since then, interest in the supernatural has remained strong. The next boom occurred during the 1960s with interest in modern witchcraft, and also fed into the 1970s as the Age of Aquarius's darker side saw the rise of Anton LeVay's counterculture group the Church of Satan and an obsession with all things dark and devilish.

ABOVE Illustrations from 1864's *Spectropia*, designed to use optical illusion to debunk spiritualism. Stare at the small asterisk in each for 25 seconds, then look at a white wall...

BELOW Illustration for MR James's *Oh, Whistle And I'll Come To You, My Lad*

"Spiritualism and the supernatural presents an age far away from ours, the Victorian age," says Natale. "You certainly see a decline in popular spiritualism since the beginning of the 20th century but this doesn't mean there was a decline in belief. Mysticism became more and more important in the 20th century and, of course, we had the New Age movement. So these beliefs don't fade away but they develop. We still have a lot of TV programmes where we can see supernatural events presented for an audience, for example *Most Haunted*, which uses the conventions of a documentary to explore haunted houses but from the perspective that it might be true. There is an underlying fascination with the supernatural and with spirits that was popularised in the 19th century."

The 19th century and the supernatural are closely linked within the public

> "Just like the spirits that so obsessed them, the Victorians' fascination with the spiritual continues to haunt us"

consciousness. Gothic horror films continue to use the Victorian manor house and the smog-filled streets of London for inspiration. Authors still evoke the atmosphere and style of writers such as MR James, with Susan Hill's 1983 novel *The Woman In Black* being a particularly strong example of the modern Victorian ghost story. And, of course, *A Christmas Carol* remains a popular yuletide fixture, with new adaptations popping up every few years. Just like the spirits that so obsessed them, the Victorians' fascination with the spiritual continues to haunt us.

PARANORMAL INVESTIGATORS

We talk to Alan Murdie, chairman of Britain's oldest ghost hunting society, The Ghost Club

What exactly is The Ghost Club and what is its mission?
The Ghost Club is essentially a private body of friends and members who are particularly interested in ghosts and the paranormal. It's a place where sceptics and believers can meet on common ground. We don't have any collective opinion, but provide a forum and meeting place where people who are interested in the subject can debate and discuss on a social basis. We also conduct our own investigations and research from time to time, looking into both the scientific and the cultural sides of ghosts and the paranormal more wildly. We primarily investigate accounts in Great Britain but we're also interested in reports of phenomena abroad. I like to think we preserve and celebrate some of our cultural traditions and history of ghosts.

Can you tell us a little about the organisation's history?
The Ghost Club's origins go back to the 1850s, to a very loose student society, which was formed at Trinity College in Cambridge. It was then launched officially in London in 1862 (with an announcement in *The Times*) and it seems to have carried on in this manner until the early 1870s, when it ceased meeting. In 1882 it was revived by Reverend Stainton Moses, a forgotten 19th century figure who combined life as a Church Of England clergyman with being a remarkable medium. The Ghost Club at this stage was a much smaller and more private body, attracting people such as Sir William Crookes and WB Yeats. They would meet every so often in London to privately discuss the latest in ghosts, but were perhaps more occult-orientated. They researched traditions and referred to each other as Brother Ghost. It continued in this manner until the 1930s, and by this time the club had begun to attract a number of significant younger researchers, such as Harry Price. Price would later become world famous for investigating Borley Rectory, a case that he worked on for 20 years and that people are still arguing about to this day. In 1938 Price then relaunched the club as a kind of society dining circle that met regularly during World War II. After Price's death in 1948, The Ghost Club suspended itself for four years until 1952, when Phillip Pool (a Fleet Street journalist) once again revived the club. That club has carried on, more or less, ever since. During the last 60-odd years The Ghost Club has typically involved investigations into allegedly haunted houses and talks by a wide range of speakers on all kinds of fascinating topics from all points of view.

The Ghost Club was founded in the 1850s

Reverend Stainton Moses revived The Ghost Club in 1882

What kind of investigations does The Ghost Club undertake?
We've conducted investigations around the country, in numerous settings, although there is one interesting exception: graveyards – we don't get many accounts of haunted graveyards these days. We have, however, looked into reports of phenomena in all kinds of domestic, public and historic buildings. These investigations are quite contrary to the sort of thing that gets televised. My predecessor Tom Perrott, who was chairman for 29 years, stated that the only equipment he took on most cases was a notebook, a pencil and a sympathetic ear. Not everything that people may think of as being paranormal is necessarily so. We had an investigation in the 1990s at the House Of Detention, which is a historic prison-turned-museum in Clerkenwell in central London, we've been into the undercroft of Battle Abbey, and then of course there's been callouts from private dwellings and houses. I've had one or two experiences during investigations, mostly involving noises or object movement that I can't explain. A number of our members do investigate things on their own account as well as with The Ghost Club, but we don't have any ghost-detecting devices. We would have solved problems in science, philosophy and theology if we did!

Religion & Belief

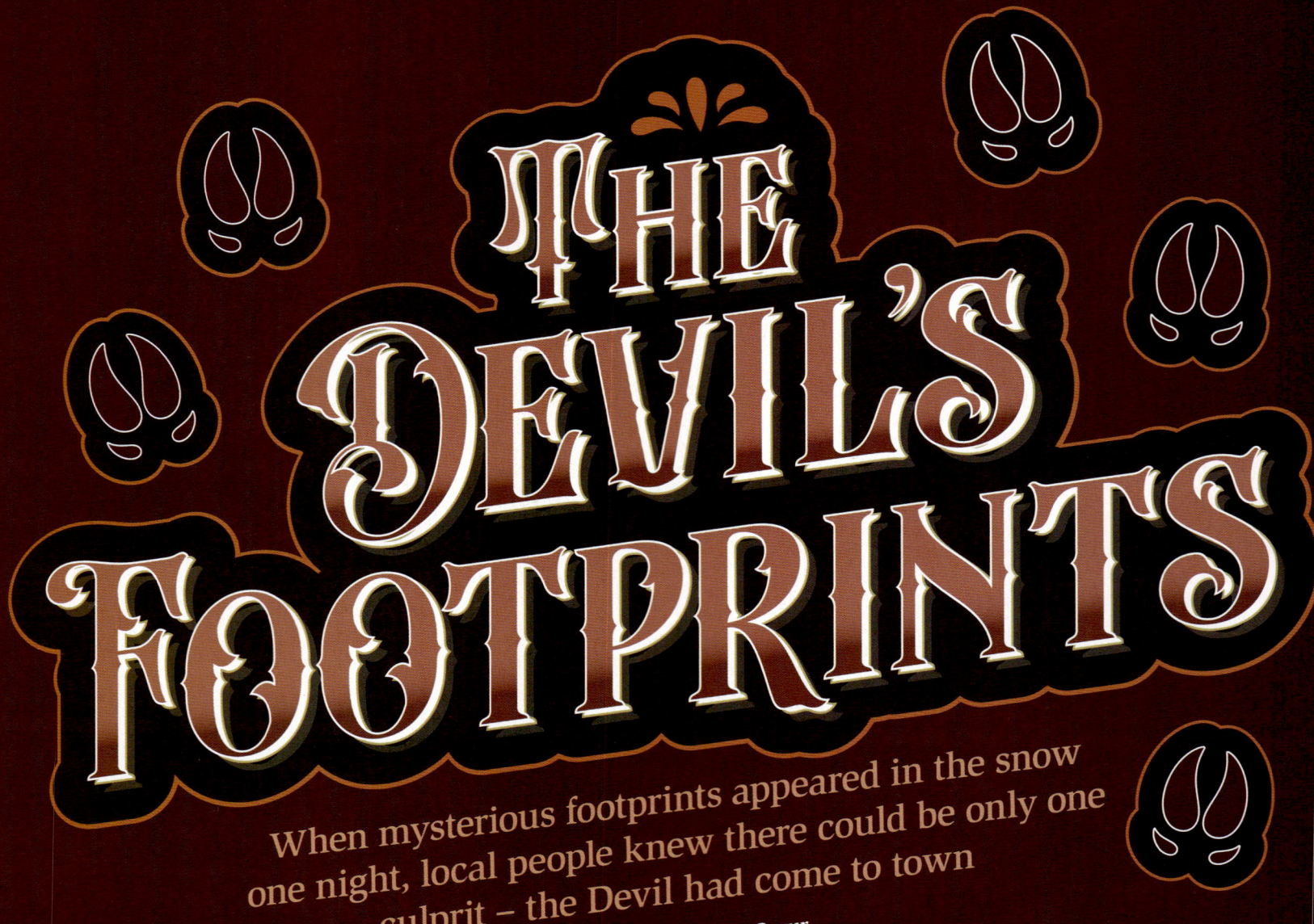

The Devil's Footprints

When mysterious footprints appeared in the snow one night, local people knew there could be only one culprit – the Devil had come to town

Written by Ben Gazur

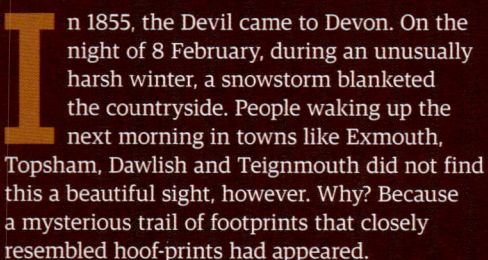

In 1855, the Devil came to Devon. On the night of 8 February, during an unusually harsh winter, a snowstorm blanketed the countryside. People waking up the next morning in towns like Exmouth, Topsham, Dawlish and Teignmouth did not find this a beautiful sight, however. Why? Because a mysterious trail of footprints that closely resembled hoof-prints had appeared.

As the newspapers of the time reported it, these devlish tracks were "the footmarks of some strange and mysterious animal endowed with the power of ubiquity, as the footprints were to be seen in all kinds of unaccountable places – on the tops of houses and narrow walls, in gardens and court-yards, enclosed by high walls and pailings, as well in open fields." For many locals the explanation for their bizarre appearance was obvious; these were the footprints of none other than the Devil himself.

The *Times*' correspondent remarked that these footprints looked as if they belonged to a biped rather than to some four-legged farm animal. Many of the tracks looked as if they had approached the doorsteps of homes before the mysterious visitor retreated. Consternation was so great that one vicar in the area drew attention to the footsteps in his sermon but suggested that instead of some supernatural event they were actually created by escaped kangaroos. Even he was not convinced by this explanation but later said that it was a useful exercise due to the terror villagers were experiencing, "dreading to go out after sunset... under the conviction that this was the Devil's work".

Some papers made merry with the event. One Exeter paper said: "We can't pretend to give an explanation of this 'mysterious affair', but all we know is that if this Devil has taken it into his head to have a steeple chase in Devon, he has manifested very peculiar taste in choosing such an inclement season for his sport."

Soon those with a more scientific leaning were keen to explain the mystery away. The famous professor Richard Owens claimed that several badgers were the culprits; others thought jumping mice might leave similar marks. One of the most novel explanations was that they were left by a balloon that was trailing its shackles along the ground. The most obvious cause, a hoofed or shod animal like a donkey, was thought unlikely due to the length of the tracks, the terrible weather and the prints' spacing.

The 1855 Devil's Footprints, therefore, remain unexplained. Intriguingly only five years earlier another track of Devil's Footprints appeared in the village of Rowley Regis – though of a quite different type. Here the footsteps were human shaped but appeared to have been burned into the ground by red-hot feet.

The Devil's Footprints

For centuries it was a common trope to show the Devil as cloven-hoofed in art, making him an obvious cause of the mysterious prints

The Devil's Footprints appeared over many miles, in many locations, and all in a single night

Though Richard Owen thought he had solved the mystery by blaming badgers, their prints do not resemble drawings of the Devil's Footprints made at the time

Religion & Belief

> During WWI, Welsh occultist Arthur Machen spawned the legend that phantom Agincourt bowmen fought at the Battle of Mons

A panel from Alphonse Mucha's illustrated *Le Pater* (*Our Father*), first published in 1899. Mucha reimagined the Lord's Prayer along occult lines, reinventing it as the individual's search for a divine state

Symbolist Belgian painter Khnoppf was commissioned by Péladan, grandmaster of Ordre de la Rose + Croix

Alphonse Mucha incorporates the 12 zodiac signs around the subject's head

The Occult Revival

As the lights dimmed on the 19th century, faith and progress broke like waves on the anxious, restless mood of the age. The dead reached out to the living, miracle cures were sought, and gurus gathered followers into secret societies

Written by James Hoare

In the summer of 1894, Sir Arthur Conan Doyle found himself in a thatched cottage on the Dorset coast. An old smuggler's haunt, it would have made the perfect seaside getaway, but the great Victorian scribe was here on business.

Appropriately for the creator of Sherlock Holmes, Doyle and his two colleagues, Frank Podmore and Dr Sydney Scott, were here to solve a mystery. They were looking for a ghost.

Like a gaslit *Most Haunted*, the trio set up with a camera and magnesium tripwire, hoping to take a photograph that would expose a spirit where the naked eye could not, but no spectral presence saw fit to glide in front of the lens.

The following night the family's 20-year-old son came to offer the investigators drinks; when they refused and began to leave, he rushed back in and begged them to stay. Suddenly there was a crashing and banging in the kitchen, as if some malevolent force were flinging open the cupboards in a rage.

The diagnosis: the son did it, with help. But over Doyle's lifetime his telling of the story changed dramatically as he became more enthused with Spiritualism – the belief the dead walk among us and can summoned – and he disowned the official report composed by his more rigorous colleagues at the Society of Psychical Research.

To the 21st century perspective it is contradictory and faintly absurd that the creator of literature's most famous rationalist could be so infamously irrational, but Doyle is a perfect example of the spirit of the age. Born a Roman Catholic and educated by Jesuits, Doyle became agnostic and then ended his life a Spiritualist. He was passionate about vaccination and briefly studied to be an ophthalmologist, but then took all manner of supernatural chicanery as a matter of faith.

The late 19th century was a period of great intellectual restlessness. The French called it 'fin de siècle', which means simply 'end of the century', but captures something that English does not; a sense of pessimism and defeat, uncertainty and frustration, decadence and immorality.

The late 18th century and much of the 19th had been defined by the relentless march of scientific progress, and society had been shaped around it; populations had decamped from the villages to the cities that were bringing new dangers and destroying old ways of life; the centuries-old supremacy of traditional religion had been winded by Charles Darwin, and political thought was dominated by the alarming new creeds of socialism and nationalism.

The social challenges posed by this collision of progress and faith were dealt with in various ways; sometimes by the rejection of one for the other, but also by the creative reconciliation of the two. In fact, the idea that the 18th-century Enlightenment gave way to inevitable secularisation is actually misleading. The truth is that the late 19th century saw belief reborn in surprising new guises.

In France, liberal Catholicism pushed for social reform, while in Britain and the United States muscular Christian activism took to the streets to change the world one tea urn at a time. In the art world, the French Symbolists drew heavily on the gothic imagery of Edgar Allan Poe to reflect imagination and reject realism, while in Germany the bombastic opera of Richard Wagner wove a new Germanic mythology with nationalist undertones and disastrous consequences for the looming 20th century. Secret societies thrived in this space where old identities – whether regional or religious – seemed uncertain.

Many were political, but others took on an occult flavour. The best known of the non-magical bunch were the Freemasons – really just an old boy's network using elaborate rituals as a social bond – who were active across much of Europe and North America, and among Britain's intellectual elite, the Society for Psychical Research stroked their chins and applied (as far

> The Symbolist movement was an influence on Carl Jung and Sigmund Freud, who used imagery to unlock the unconscious

91

Religion & Belief

Spooks and charlatans

From the very beginnings of Spiritualism, some of its practitioners were being outed as frauds who took advantage of the bereaved.

The movement began in rural New York with Margaret and Kate Fox, two sisters who in 1848 convinced their older sister their home was haunted by rapping the floor with an apple on a piece of string. They soon took what was effectively their circus act on the road with the help of some trusting Quakers who formed the core of the new Spiritualist movement.

Though the Fox sisters were outed and confessed in 1888, their dubious craft continued through countless others who used hidden accomplices, fake arms, or string to move objects, and double exposure to create haunting 'spirit photographs' that exposed spectral visitors where none had been previously visible.

The fraudulent Spiritualists had their opponents though and faced condemnation from some religious authorities, were subject to vigorous testing by the Society of Physical Research, and were dogged by the illusionist Harry Houdini, who recognised a perversion of his own craft at work.

Though he was an old friend of Arthur Conan Doyle, Houdini and Doyle began to trade blows in the press as Houdini campaigned to expose Spiritualists by touring a stage show in which he replicated their tricks.

---

as they were concerned) rigorous scientific study to debate the veracity of poltergeists and spiritual or demonic possessions.

Some secret societies were contemporary reimaginings of older branches of Christian mysticism – the Martinists, Templars and Rosicrucians, and their myriad variants, schisms and spin-offs – but hot on their heels came new sects that cribbed notes from their holier-than-thou predecessors and created something dynamic and new, that would redefine occultism outside of Scripture's shadow.

Most notable of these was the Hermetic Order of the Golden Dawn, and, under Britain's infamous Aleister Crowley, the previously benign Ordo Templi Orientis (OTO). OTO had its origins as a German response to Freemasonry, but morphed into the vessel for Crowley's new faith, Thelema, in the first decade of the 20th century.

Another world unto itself was the Theosophical Society, founded in the US by a Russian emigré Spiritualist called Helena Blavatsky. From her beginnings as a fraudulent table-tapper, Madame Blavatsky had become increasingly enthused by Hindu and Buddhist thought and from the 1880s the Theosophical Society – which relocated its HQ to India – became focused on attaining higher states of consciousness by following the esoteric learning of the Masters of the Ancient Wisdom, who had been helpfully reincarnated into the club's upper echelons.

The abrasive German philosopher Friedrich Nietzsche explained it best, writing in 1872's *The Birth of Tragedy*:

"What does our great historic hunger signify, our clutching about us for countless other cultures, our consuming desire for knowledge if not the loss of myth, the mythic home, the mythic womb?"

In the German-speaking world the search for a "mythic womb" was especially potent and the völkisch ('folkish') movement emerged in the early 19th century and morphed – thanks to the influence of Theosophy – into Armanism or Ariosophy in the 1890s. Austrian antiquarians Guido von List and Jörg Lanz von Liebenfels believed there was a spiritual link between the Germanic people and their land, and the ancient Germans were a nobler and purer bunch before the arrival of "foreign" influences like Christianity, industrialisation, and democracy, as well as "foreign" races like Slavs and Jews.

This unique combination of elements, albeit with an Irish-republican rather than virulently racist character, would emerge outside of Germany in the Celtic Revival poetry of WB Yeats, a rare romantic nationalist in London's occult ecosystem of glorified gentlemen's supper clubs, as well as his fellow Irishmen, the artist and poet George William "AE" Russell, and the fantasy novelist Lord Dunsany.

"I often think I would put this belief in magic from me if I could," wrote Yeats somewhat bitterly in his 1903 pamphlet, *Ideas of Good and Evil*, "for I have come to see or to imagine, in men and women, in houses, in handicrafts, in nearly all sights and sounds, a certain evil, a certain ugliness, that comes from the slow perishing through the centuries of a quality of mind that made this belief and its evidences common over the world."

Harry Houdini pulls no punches in this 1909 poster for his medium-busting stage show

Light radiates from the forehead of Alphonse Mucha's Morning Star

> After demonstrating her powers in India, Helena Blavatsky was exposed as a fraud in 1885 by the Society for Psychical Research

92

The Occult Revival

Newmann the Great was a renowned hypnotist in the United States

> Upset by the growing scepticism of the Society for Psychical Research, Sir Arthur Conan Doyle led a mass resignation

In contrast to this nationalist primitivism, French occultism was largely a metropolitan affair not much bothered by a retreat into wilderness or a narrow-eyed suspicion of the modern world. It was defined broadly by prayer and absinthe, for those not quite ready to cut their strings to Mother Church and the decadent dandies-about-town.

Symbolism was an art movement inspired by the writer Charles Baudelaire. He translated Edgar Allan Poe into French and sought to find through his work the au-delà – the world beyond our own – with the routes available to this lusty band being dreams, substance abuse, sex and the occult.

Among their number were artists Fernand Khnopff, Jan Toorop and Jean Delville, and writers André Gide, Stephane Mallarmé, and Joris-Karl Huysmans, a Benedictine lay brother turned mystical novelist. Over the fence in Art Nouveau, the Paris-resident Czech artist Alphonse Mucha dabbled in Theosophy and occultism, and conjured mythic, folkloric figures in his stylised, dreamlike work.

Catholic apostasy provided France with its most dramatic characters, often rooted in Martinism (a belief that man could return to the spiritual state of grace he had enjoyed in the Garden of Eden), Gnosticism (belief that the physical world is debased but man can ascend in spirit) or the Kabbalah (Jewish mysticism based on the power of the Hebrew alphabet and numerals), or all three.

These included the jailbird and former seminary student Éliphas Lévi, credited as the father of modern occultism, and the flamboyant figure of Joséphin Péladan, who called himself Le Sâr – the Babylonian title for king. Péladan was ostensibly a Martinist, but built bridges by resurrecting the Rosicrucian Brotherhood

The Sphinx is Khnoppf's best-known work and depicts Oedipus nestled next to the eponymous creature

A New Dawn

No other organisation conjures up such feverish imaginings, was associated with so many larger than life characters (not all of whom were actually members), nor played such a vital role in transitioning the occult from the late 19th century and into the 20th as the Hermetic Order of the Golden Dawn.

The origin story is a bit of a fog of self-mythologising courtesy of some of its more infamous members such as Aleister Crowley, but what we know for fact is that the Golden Dawn was founded in 1887 by Samuel Liddell MacGregor Mathers, William Robert Woodman and William Wynn Westcott, based on a what they claimed was a recently deciphered Rosicrucian manuscript. The duo dutifully built their new society around the rituals contained within, which they insisted – dubiously – to be of ancient Egyptian origin.

Lineage was incredibly important to late 19th century occultists, but their influences were more recent and that's what made the Golden Dawn such a potent distillation of the entire occult revival to date. It liberally helped itself to elements of theosophy, cosmology, Kabbalah rituals, astrology, alchemy, astral travel and the tarot, and Byzantine Rosicrucian rites and initiations.

Unlike earlier orders, the focus of the Golden Dawn was on practical magic and ritual, and so it found itself attracting the hungriest and most ambitious of occultists. These fiercely intelligent and competitive intellectuals thrived in the hierarchy of different ranks and levels, and – especially Crowley – had a marvellous time pulling the society apart in 1903.

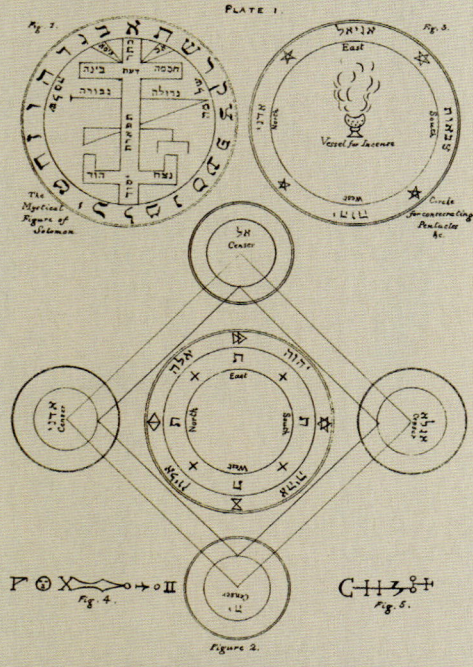

Kabbalist sigils from Samuel Liddell MacGregor Mathers' translation of the Renaissance grimoire *The Key of Solomon*

93

Religion & Belief

"Magic didn't mean a retreat from Christianity, nor was it in opposition to scientific thinking"

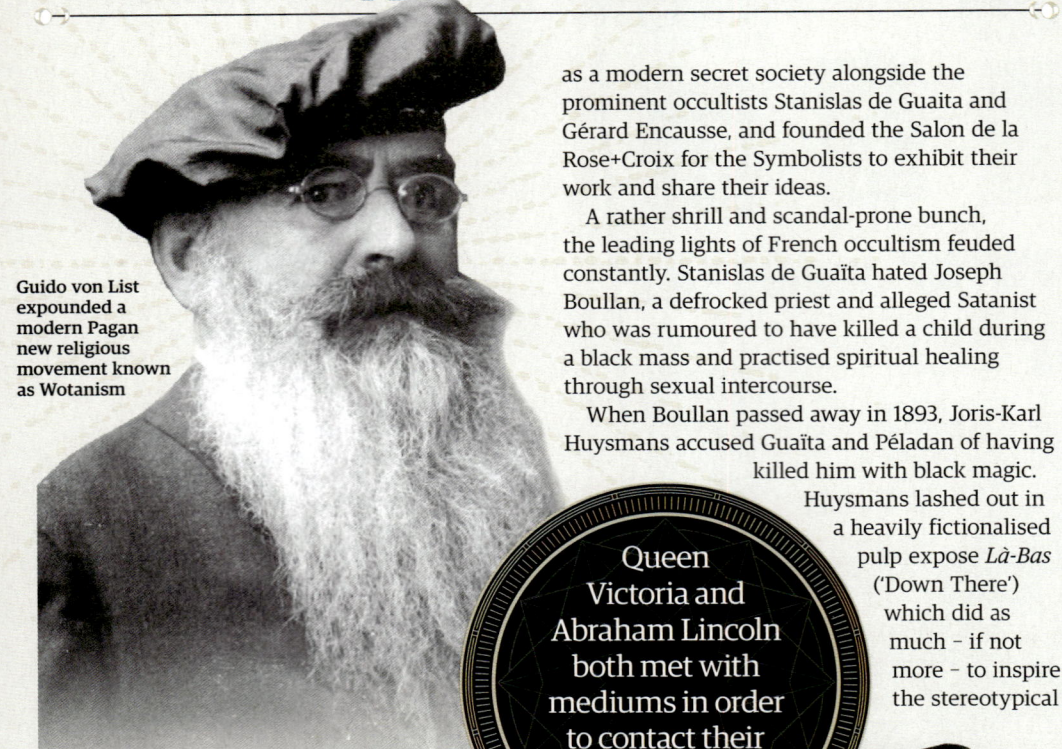

Guido von List expounded a modern Pagan new religious movement known as Wotanism

Double exposure creates the illusion of a ghost hovering over an elderly couple

as a modern secret society alongside the prominent occultists Stanislas de Guaïta and Gérard Encausse, and founded the Salon de la Rose+Croix for the Symbolists to exhibit their work and share their ideas.

A rather shrill and scandal-prone bunch, the leading lights of French occultism feuded constantly. Stanislas de Guaïta hated Joseph Boullan, a defrocked priest and alleged Satanist who was rumoured to have killed a child during a black mass and practised spiritual healing through sexual intercourse.

When Boullan passed away in 1893, Joris-Karl Huysmans accused Guaïta and Péladan of having killed him with black magic. Huysmans lashed out in a heavily fictionalised pulp expose *Là-Bas* ('Down There') which did as much – if not more – to inspire the stereotypical look of Satanism than anything that real occultists ever did.

Just as magic didn't necessarily mean a retreat from Christianity, nor was it necessarily in opposition to scientific thinking. Instead the occult was another means to interpret a world that was only just beginning to be understood in any real kind of detail. In a sense too, the growing confidence of the scientific worldview in tipping over the old certainties left what remained indecipherable up for grabs by concepts that seemed just as esoteric to the layman as bacteria or electrons.

Art movements love a good manifesto, and so the Belgian Symbolist Jean Delville spared few words in explaining his worldview in 1900's *New Mission in Art*:

"The occult sciences, the lofty teachings of theosophy, and experimental Spiritualism, are setting out to conquer the future, and, on the threshold of a new age, are about to establish the Science of the Ideal; that is the synthesis of science, religion, and philosophy."

Some ideas clung so close to science that they still wear its cast-offs as pseudoscience or parapsychology, chief among them the doctrines of Spiritualism and mesmerism.

Mesmerism wasn't just hypnosis by another name. This art – the same one by which wandering holy man Grigori Rasputin claimed to be able to stem the internal bleeding of poor bloody Alexei, ill-fated heir to the Russian throne – was based on the premise that all living beings were governed by magnetic forces. The word "mesmerise" takes its name from its inventor, the 18th century German physician Franz Anton Mesmer who also coined "animal magnetism", not to refer to physical attraction but the pull of celestial bodies on living creatures.

Through the use of magnetised wands and other props, the practitioner could claim to cure the vaguely defined health issues that have always been

> Queen Victoria and Abraham Lincoln both met with mediums in order to contact their deceased loved ones

Mesmerism was a well established form of music hall entertainment

Péladan's *Le vice suprême* was interwoven with Rosicrucian and occult themes

The Occult Revival

A séance appears to have attracted a ghostly visitor

In March 1890 W B Yeats joined the Hermetic Order of the Golden Dawn

The Gods Delusion

An ironic consequence of the scientific method was the idea that folklore and superstition represented a glimpse of pre-Christian religious practices, an essentially flawed premise that actually birthed new belief systems across the late 19th and early 20th century.

Anthropology emerged as a discipline in the mid-1800s and Europe's overseas empires offered an opportunity for inquiring minds to understand the nature of belief among what they once called the 'savages'.

Religion was organised and classified like insects under glass in an act of linear Eurocentric evolution in which fetishism (the imbuing of physical objects or locations with religious importance) gave way to polytheism (belief in multiple deities) which in turn gave way to monotheism (belief in a single deity), which was finally superseded by science.

The anthropologist Edward Burnett Tylor coined the idea of "survivals" in 1871, proposing that folklore, ritual and superstition was in fact a remnant of earlier belief systems. Tylor's theory prompted a flurry of folklore collection and study, most infamously in 13 volumes of Sir James Frazer's *The Golden Bough: A Study in Comparative Religion*, which were published between 1892 and 1913. (It was re-subtitled *A Study in Magic and Religion* in its second and subsequent editions.)

Frazer's hastily drawn conclusions and cherry-picking research would prove profoundly influential in underscoring the alleged commonalities of pre-Christian mythology, and through the so-called "survivals", inviting occultists to recreate "old religions" – some of which never really existed or about which archaeologists still know precious little.

Scottish anthropologist Sir James George Frazer, author of The Golden Bough

---

fair game for quacks. Though quickly discredited, it lived on in the imagination of occultists and had a second wind from 1841 when Scottish surgeon James Braid certified the veracity of a French mesmerist's act and became convinced that suggestion was more important than magnets – which was spot on, although not in the way he thought – and replaced it with hypnotism.

Thanks to Braid, mesmerism not only became an established part of medical orthodoxy as both a sedative and means of prompting the body to heal itself, but returned to music halls and dinner parties as a popular phenomenon.

Spiritualism was born in the United States in the 1850s. It existed independently of much of the day's occult milieu, and despite a crossover in interest, it captured the public imagination in a way that ritual magic and esoteric secret societies failed to, dominating theatres with seances in which mediums purported to receive messages from dead loved ones. Lights dimmed, tables rattled and 'ectoplasm' was vomited forth by the unknown, unseen ghostly entities that had apparently been summoned.

Curiously, while much of this history has been dominated by men, Spiritualism was incredibly popular with women and many of the practising mediums were female. Indeed, the only woman mentioned so far – Helena Blavatsky – started out as a Spiritualist.

> Charles Henry Allan Bennett was more interested in enlightenment, and established the first Buddhist mission in Britain

For many though, spiritualism conjures up one name, that of its most ardent evangelist: Sir Arthur Conan Doyle. Though his forthright position on the supernatural dealt a hammer blow to his credibility later in his career, in the context of the late 19th century at least, there was little remarkable, contradictory or at the time even remotely controversial about his passions.

"There is nothing scientifically impossible," he wrote, in defence of the fraudulent photographs of the Cottingley Fairies, which he believed in wholeheartedly, "so far as I can see, in some people seeing things that are invisible to others."

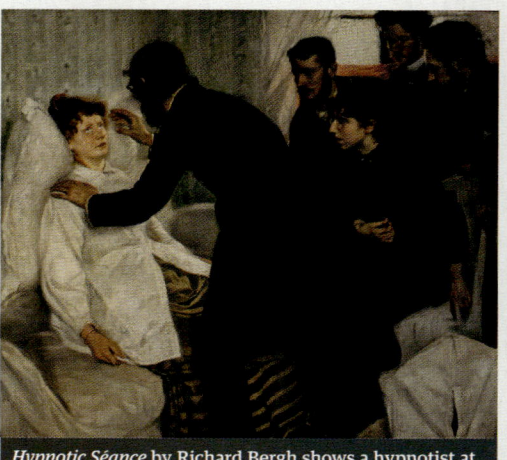

Hypnotic Séance by Richard Bergh shows a hypnotist at work in front of a rapt audience

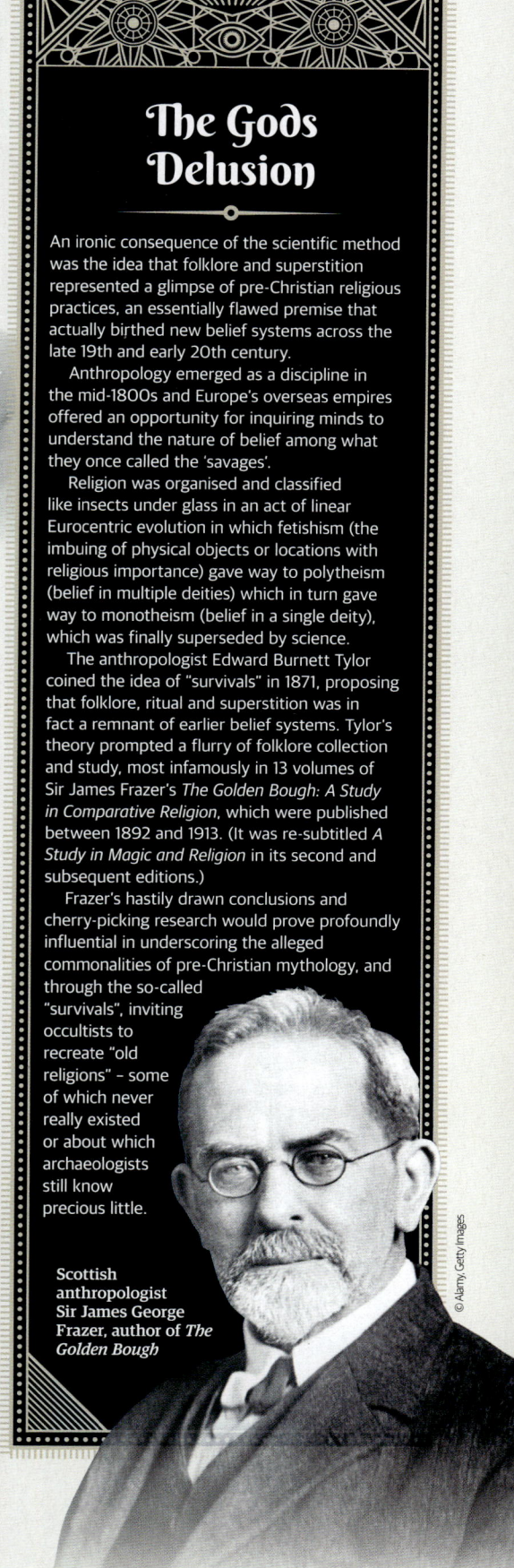

95

Religion & Belief

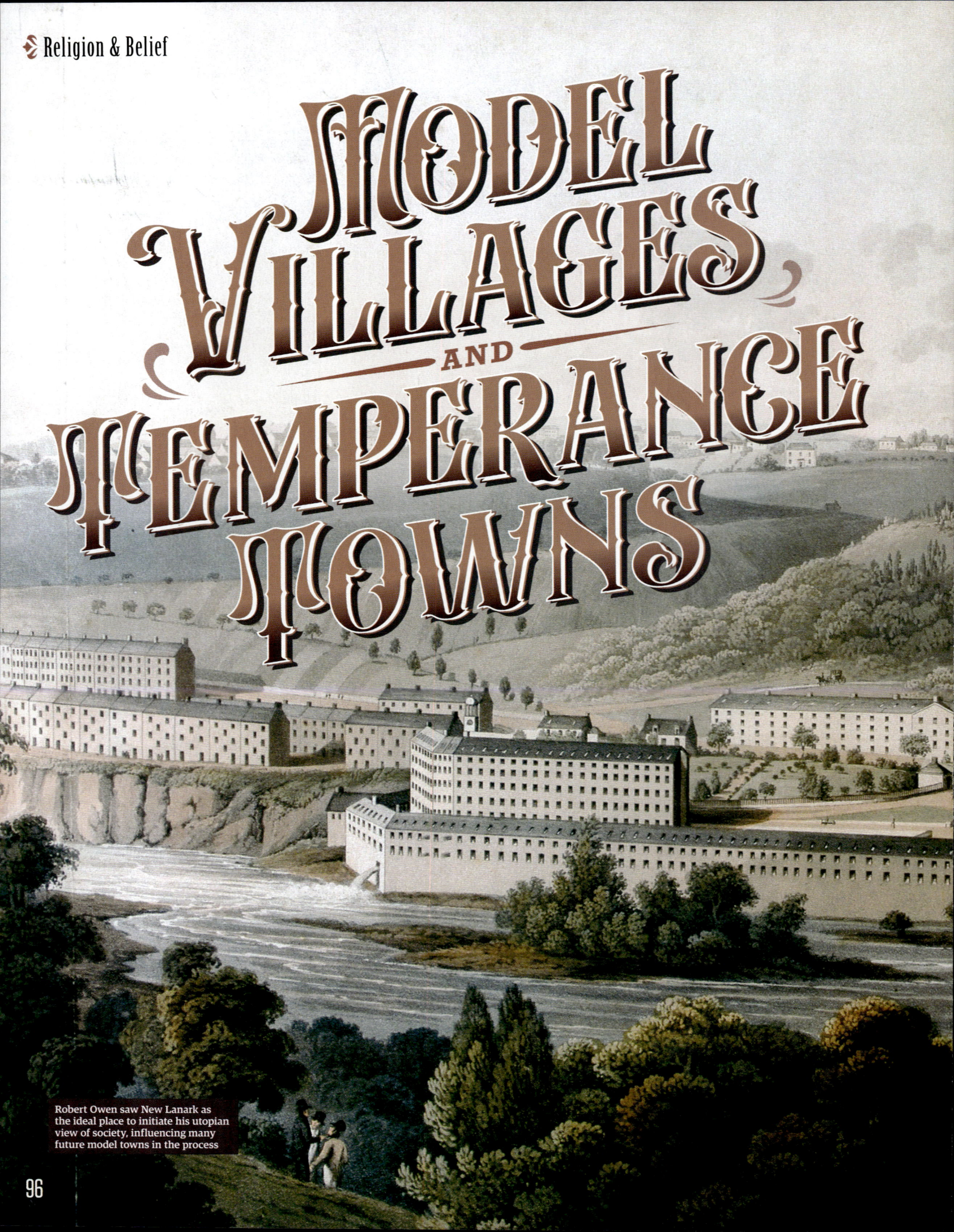

MODEL VILLAGES AND TEMPERANCE TOWNS

Robert Owen saw New Lanark as the ideal place to initiate his utopian view of society, influencing many future model towns in the process

Model Villages and Temperance Towns

In order to boost productivity – and control behaviour and morality – company owners moved their workforce out of crowded cities and into all-new purpose-built towns

Written by Jack Griffiths

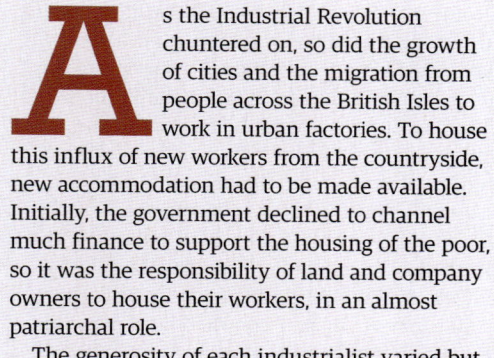

As the Industrial Revolution chuntered on, so did the growth of cities and the migration from people across the British Isles to work in urban factories. To house this influx of new workers from the countryside, new accommodation had to be made available. Initially, the government declined to channel much finance to support the housing of the poor, so it was the responsibility of land and company owners to house their workers, in an almost patriarchal role.

The generosity of each industrialist varied but, in the minds of many factory owners, the aim was to house as many workers as cheaply and quickly as possible. What followed was an expansion of the traditional method of owners housing their staff in farms and mills. This was the birth of 'model towns' – all new communities built close to the factories. In city slums, the quality and comfort of the housing was often poor. Sometimes damp or cold, and sometimes both, these houses rarely had running water and were shared by several families of workers. The interiors of the houses were arranged so as many people could squeeze in as possible. Often they were simple one-up one-down terraces but workers could also rent rooms or even cellars in larger houses. With little or no outside space, and shared toilets, the damp close-quarters encouraged the spread of disease. Bread, potatoes and tea were the staple foods, along with meat on occasion, but this low-vitamin diet could cause malnutrition, which would then develop into diseases like scurvy and rickets. Factory owners developed the concept of the model town to improve these conditions of squalor experienced by urban dwellers in non-company housing across British cities. These model towns would be built away from the choking smog of city centre industry. The correlation had been made that healthier and happier workers, living and sleeping in the shadow of the very factory they worked in, would be more productive for business.

With the workforce being housed in the same location, residents could attend purpose-built communal schools, outside spaces and churches. Many of the small houses weren't equipped with cooking facilities or storage space, so the workers were reliant on fresh food deliveries by the company. Model towns were only feasible due to the growth of the railways. This developing network allowed for quicker transport of cargo to construct and build the towns, as well as people

> **"FACTORY OWNERS DEVELOPED THE CONCEPT OF THE MODEL TOWN TO IMPROVE CONDITIONS OF SQUALOR EXPERIENCED BY URBAN DWELLERS IN NON-COMPANY HOUSING"**

Religion & Belief

to live and work in them. Royalty even briefly became involved with Prince Albert interested in this revolution of house building for the poor with his so-called 'model dwelling'. This property was put on display at London's 1851 Great Exhibition and was designed as a model cottage for the working class to live in that would be healthier than usual slum accommodation.

A major player in this first instance of widespread development of social housing was Titus Salt. Salt, a kingpin in the Bradford textile industry in the 1850s, planned the construction of Saltaire, a new village that would be constructed near the city to house workers to work in its mills. The town takes its name from its founder and the river Aire, which flows through it and forms part of the Leeds to Liverpool canal. Focusing his efforts on a healthier more-efficient workforce, he moved his base of operations out of Bradford to this new planned community. It took around 25 years to complete and didn't skimp on the amenities. Its more than 800 homes had access to churches, a school and a park and even a hospital and baths.

Salt was a pioneer, his innovation influencing many more business owners to place more of an emphasis on town planning. Two of these were the brothers George and Richard Cadbury, owners of the famous confectionery company, who relocated their factory out of Birmingham and into Worcestershire in an effort to boost productivity and sales. Named after the nearby river, Bourn, Bournville was a 49 hectare (120-acre) model town with numbers of cottages built for the Cadbury employees along with leisure and sports areas for exercise and gardens to grow fresh vegetables. Better still, this Bournville was well-linked to canals and railways and workers could even take part in summer camps at the on-site lido. Bournville continued to grow as the company prospered, with more than 300 dwellings by 1900, and it is still there to this day.

With no building regulations, city landowners and builders often tried to fit as many people in on the smallest plot of land possible

Bournville was such a success that many other individuals and companies followed suit. Away from model towns, there was also reform underway back in the cities. Octavia Hill was a social reformer and the founder of the National Trust. She took it upon herself to improve dilapidated housing in London through shrewd management. She made a concentrated effort to strike up relationships with the working class renters so there could be a two-way conversation between landowner and tenant on how to improve living standards. George Peabody was another who recognised the value of hygiene to health. In his buildings, he ensured that there were separate baths and laundries as well as playgrounds for children. He also based his model dwellings around an open square, making areas more spacious and light, a marked improvement to dark cramped alleys.

Over the border in Wales, Tremadog was a planned settlement created to help lessen poverty. The area was drained to make it stable

NEW LANARK: SCOTLAND'S MOST FAMOUS MODEL TOWN

Conceived as a socialist utopia, Robert Owen's planned settlement would influence later urban planning developments

New Lanark was founded in 1785 but it wasn't until the next century that its growth and success accelerated. Its founder was David Dale but it was his son-in-law, Welshman Robert Owen, who oversaw its expansion into an idealistic model town. A village centred around cotton mills, Owen grasped the opportunity to develop the area on the banks of the River Clyde, in the vicinity of both Glasgow and Edinburgh. His vision was for a model community which was purpose-built to support industry, while being comfortable and spacious for its inhabitants. He assumed ownership of the area's mills and revitalised New Lanark in accordance with his socialist philosophy. He installed a focus on education and welfare and reformed the factories to bring them up to standard. He introduced progressive measures including decreasing the working day from 11 to 10.5 hours and banning children under 10-years-old from working and instead providing them with nursery and schooling. Owen described the town as "the most important experiment for the happiness of the human race that has yet been instituted in any part of the world". A big claim but it did indeed form the basis of the model towns that were to come later in the Victorian period.

Since 2001, New Lanark has been a UNESCO World Heritage site after the last mill stopped spinning in 1968

Model Villages and Temperance Towns

Bournville was purpose-built to house, and to ensure the workers of Cadbury, the famous Midlands confectionary company, were as productive as possible

> "AN ADDED INCENTIVE TO CREATING MODEL TOWNS WAS TO QUELL WHAT THEY SAW AS HIGH-LEVELS OF DRINKING AMONGST WORKERS"

for construction and soon cottages and a market square took form along with a town hall and a church. This set the scene for industry to move in with one of the first woollen mills in Wales opening, as well as a new train station to support the fast-growing town. Another planned settlement in Wales was Elan Valley. Unlike Tremadog, it was specifically built for, and populated by, workers who were building new dams and reservoirs in the country. On entry to Elan Valley, employees underwent a medical to ensure they were healthy and wouldn't spread diseases through the workforce. After the Acts of the Union in 1800 brought Britain and Ireland together, model town ideas spread over the Irish Sea as well, with the construction of Portlaw, Sion Mills and Bessbrook. Port Sunlight was a town created for workers at the Sunlight soap factory, which had a concert hall, an art gallery and even a temperance hotel, where no alcohol was served.

An added incentive for industrialists, philanthropists and governments to create model towns, was to quell what they saw as high-levels of drinking amongst workers. The consumption of alcohol decreased productivity levels and drunkenness could cause brawls and anti-social behaviour. Cynics believed that this focus on alcohol allowed owners to ignore other issues such as overcrowding in houses and poor working conditions but, nonetheless, groups were set up to discourage drinking as part of a temperance movement. The movement involved a number of groups in different cities meeting and speaking about the problems with alcohol and drunkenness. Initial guidance encouraged the drinking of beer rather than harder liquor like gin. The Beer Act of 1830 made it easier to sell beer at the expense of gin to avoid any relapses of the gin crazes of the past century. The movement soon went further with the promotion of complete teetotalism and even totally dry towns. These temperance towns banned the sale and consumption of alcohol within their limits. One example was in an inner-city suburb of Cardiff. Built in the 1860s, any alcoholic trade was forbidden by the teetotal landowner, as was the construction of any public houses. Many temperance towns would later be established in the Prohibition era of the USA in the 1920s and 30s. Elan Valley tried a different approach. Although the sale of alcohol was permitted, it was strictly only available in one licensed canteen and the profits were put straight back into the community's hospital and school.

The success of these model towns and the individual philanthropists that funded them, helped usher in the 1890 Housing Act. Now, with the formation of county and district councils, local authorities had the power and appetite to build more accommodation for working class renters, that was more affordable on their salaries and were more hygienic and spacious than slum housing. The knowledge and willingness to provide better housing enabled more people to move to towns as Britain continued to urbanise. Model towns also sowed the seeds for the Garden City Movement, Ebenezer Howard's future vision for a more modern type of town and city.

Saltaire is now a UNESCO World Heritage Site, featuring shops and restaurants, as well as the original buildings, complete with the Victorian architecture of the time

99

Industry & Invention

100

Contents

Industry & Invention

102 The spirit of invention
110 **Scheele's green: The dye of death**
112 Twilight sleep
114 **The eye of the beholder**
118 The golden age of taxidermy
120 **CSI Whitechapel**
126 The everlasting staircase
128 **The Crystal Palace**

Industry & Invention

THE SPIRIT OF INVENTION

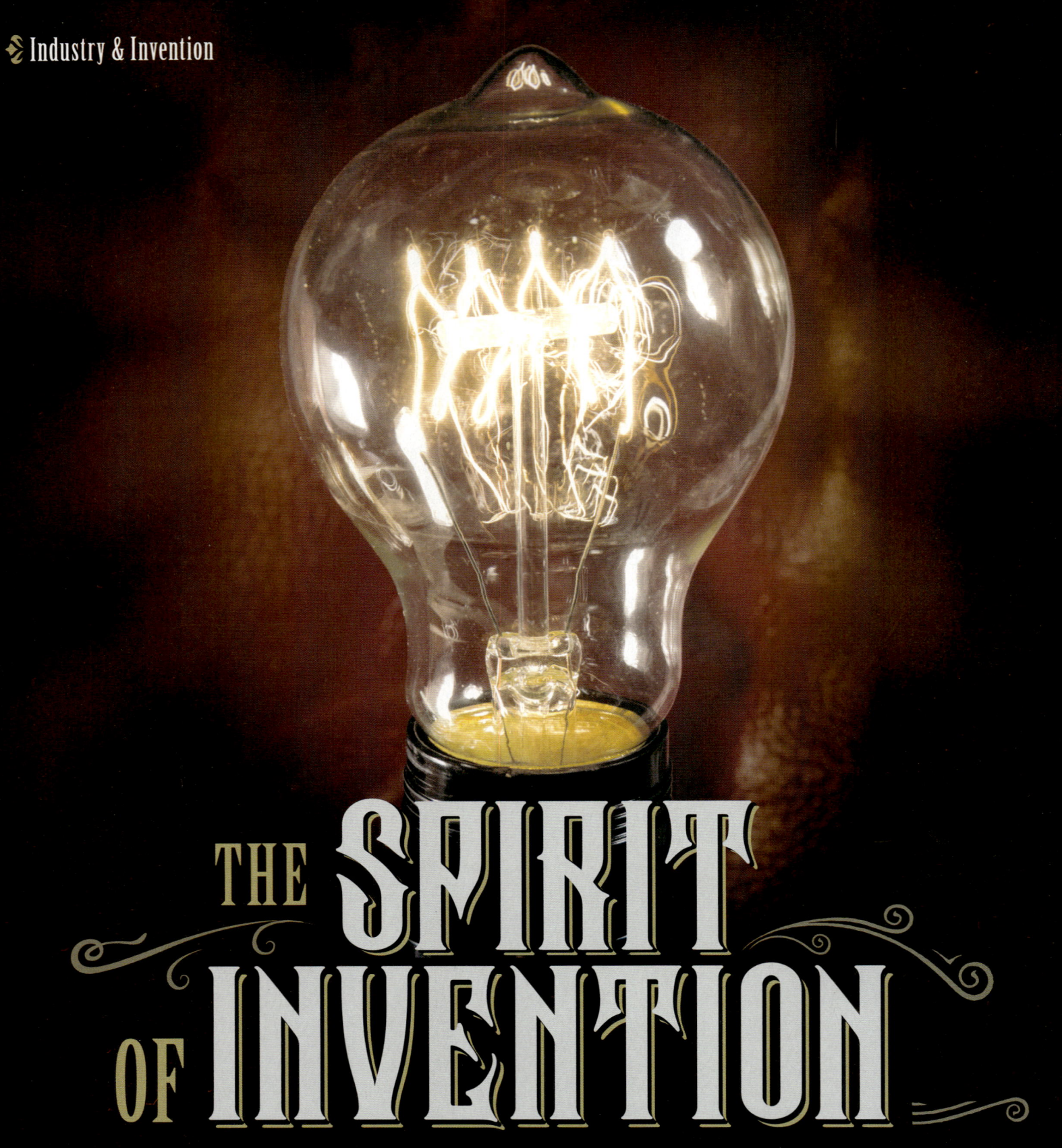

In a setting of vast change, the contagious spirit of invention was gaining momentum and inspiring the nation's most brilliant minds

The air was heavy with the smog of the Industrial Revolution as Britain chugged and clinked with newfangled machinery. It marked a period where major technological developments hugely enhanced the standard of living and set the groundwork for today's somewhat sleeker gadgetry.

By the 1830s, first-world countries were powered by steam and built with iron; there were engines, bridges and trains in drains. Elsewhere, advances in medicine were coming thick and fast. There were tablets that would ease pain and ether that would remove it entirely. A surgical operation was no longer something to consider committing suicide over. Mortality rates fell and Europe's population doubled during the 19th century to 400 million.

Among the life-saving inventions were those that enabled communication and home improvements that made life a little easier. Here you'll find the best of the best, as well as the stories of how they came to life in what was a fascinating time in history.

MEDICINE

ANAESTHETIC

Before anaesthetic, the ancient Greeks would use herbal concoctions in a bid to reduce the stress of medical procedures. The word itself is Greek, meaning 'without sensation', but this wasn't coined until 1846 when poet and physician Oliver Wendell Holmes referred to a new technique he'd witnessed, where a patient was given ether before having a tumour painlessly removed.

Ether had existed for hundreds of years, but no one had thought to use it as an anaesthetic until former dental student William Morton began experimenting in secret on small animals and even himself. Until then, students had been inhaling ether fumes for fun, dubbed 'ether frolics', where people would lose control of their motor functions and incur cuts and bruises without feeling any pain.

Gone were the days of plying patients with alcohol and opium, commanding several men to pin them down as the scalpel made contact with flesh. Deaths were avoided as surgeons were able to take more time operating and, in return, more medical discoveries were made.

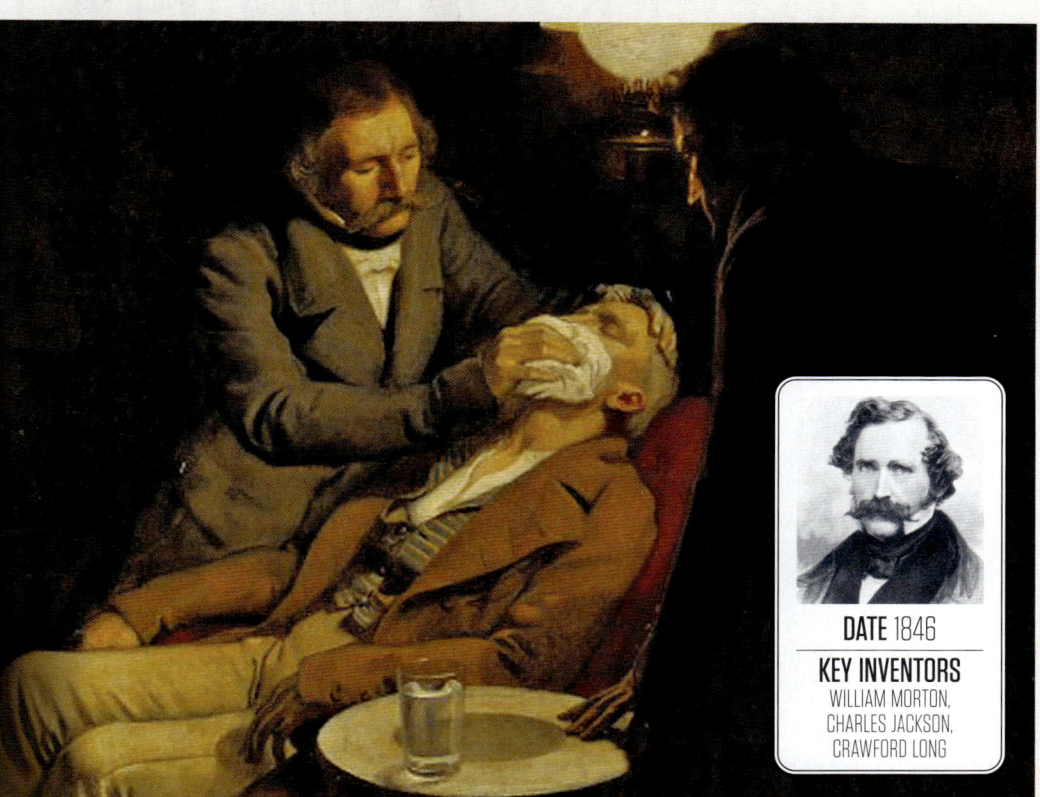

DATE 1846
KEY INVENTORS WILLIAM MORTON, CHARLES JACKSON, CRAWFORD LONG

ASPIRIN

Aspirin is one of the most successful over-the-counter pain remedies of all time, with new benefits constantly being uncovered. It was one of the first drugs to be made available in tablet form, which isn't surprising when you consider that the natural form of aspirin is found in plants such as willow and myrtle and had been used for easing pain for centuries. In 400 BCE, Greek physicians were serving women willow leaf tea during childbirth and in 1763 a reverend in England was dishing out dried willow bark to sufferers of rheumatic fever.

But it wasn't until the Victorian era that it went beyond a herbal folk medicine, as salicylic acid was made from the active ingredient in willow by French scientists. Further tweaking was needed, though, since it left many upset stomachs in its wake. German scientists created a more stable and palatable form in 1897 and aspirin was launched two years later. It took thousands of minds from across the world to develop this natural remedy and refine it into a potentially life-saving preventive tablet.

DATE 1899
KEY INVENTORS CHARLES FREDRIC, FELIX HOFFMANN

X-RAY

Ever wondered what the 'X' in X-ray stands for? You might be disappointed to learn that even its inventor, German physicist Wilhelm Röntgen, didn't know. While experimenting by passing electrical currents through a cathode tube filled with a special gas, he discovered the tube produced a glow. It seemed he had discovered an invisible light that he didn't fully understand, so he called it 'X-radiation', because in maths, 'X' is used to represent an unknown value.

Röntgen didn't stop there, even drafting in his wife and producing the first X-ray photo of her hand. News travelled fast throughout the world, and scientists were soon able to replicate and refine X-ray images.

Röntgen's belief that scientific discoveries belonged to the world kept him from patenting his invention and the medical community embraced his discovery. Making fractures, bullets and foreign bodies visible for all to see, the X-ray transformed medicine. Röntgen shied away from his newfound fame, but his breakthrough was celebrated the world over and he was eventually awarded the first Nobel Prize in Physics.

DATE 1895
KEY INVENTORS WILHELM RÖNTGEN

The Spirit of Invention

Industry & Invention

TRANSPORTATION

AUTOMOBILE

Steam-powered automobiles had been developed in the late-18th century, and in 1807 a French inventor patented a design for a car powered by an internal combustion engine. But the first truly 'modern' automobile was Karl Benz's Patent-Motorwagen. The three-wheeled vehicle had a single-cylinder four-stroke engine, which ran on petrol and produced about 2/3 horsepower at 250 rpm. Benz patented it in 1886, after which he unveiled his innovative new creation to the public. The 'horseless carriage' was written off as a fad; a dangerous weapon that would be a 'menace' to the streets. But in 1888, Benz's wife Bertha did something to change all that. Supposedly without her husband's knowledge, Bertha took the Motorwagen and embarked on a 194km-round trip from Mannheim to her hometown of Pforzheim, and in doing so carried out the first long-distance automobile journey. She had proved it fit for daily use, and so the Benz became the first 'production' vehicle.

A three-wheeeled vehicle with a horizontal single cylinder motor designed by Carl Benz

DATE 1886
KEY INVENTORS
KARL BENZ, ENRICO BERNARDI, FREDERICK LANCHESTER

SUSPENSION BRIDGE

The famous inventor, designer and engineer Isambard Kingdom Brunel was a huge part of Britain's Industrial Revolution, building bridges, tunnels, railways, docks and ships. He changed the way people could travel and many of his designs still stand today, such as London's Paddington Station (1854) and the Clifton Suspension Bridge in Bristol.

The latter was a wrought-iron marvel, linking Clifton in Bristol to Leigh Woods in North Somerset, England. It also marked Brunel's first commission. It was the earliest of its kind, high enough so that tall ships could sail beneath it and sturdy enough to provide safe passage for pedestrians and horse-drawn carriages. Unfortunately, due to the Bristol riots, the bridge wasn't built until after his death but this distinctive landmark served as a fitting memorial to the great man.

DATE 1864
KEY INVENTORS
ISAMBARD KINGDOM BRUNEL

The Spirit of Invention

DATE 1863
KEY INVENTORS
CHARLES PEARSON

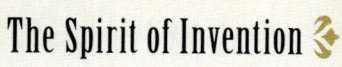

LONDON UNDERGROUND

Trains were a popular way to travel in the Victorian era, undercutting the cost of a horse-drawn carriage and beating it to the finish line, too. But the rise in Greater London's population meant the city was beginning to buckle under the strain of too many commuters and not enough transport links to get them where they needed to be. Then Charles Pearson proposed a plan to move everything underground, the so-called 'train in a drain', in 1845. It took some persuading but the House of Commons approved a bill in 1853 to build a subterranean railway from Paddington to Farringdon. It was over 150 years ago that the world's first underground train made its debut journey, with passengers anxious to experience it.

The Metropolitan was a huge success and 26,000 people hopped aboard each day in the first six months. However, it wasn't just the gap they had to mind, as commuters were enveloped in clouds of smoke from the steam trains and other passengers (smoking wasn't banned until after the King's Cross fire in 1987). The Underground continued to grow, reaching out to the then sleepy villages of Hammersmith and Morden and the transport links caused their modest populations to boom. Charles Pearson never lived to see his vision completed, having died a year before the Underground opened, but his legacy is everlasting.

The London Underground is the world's oldest subway system

Industry & Invention

COMMUNICATION

RADIO

Italian inventor Guglielmo Marconi had heard about the existence of so-called radio waves that travel through the air and it made him wonder whether sound could travel the same way, via air waves.

He built two machines, one that could transmit messages and another that could receive them and managed to make a bell ring across the room using this method. Excited by his initial success, he worked on increasing the distance but no one wanted to invest to help him develop his machines, so he moved to Britain where his technology was welcomed by the army and the Post Office. He registered for a patent in 1901, then set about making a radio wave transmitter and a receiver to convert the waves into electricity, which then turned into sound. The first signals he was able to send were in Morse code, but this vital discovery would later develop the ability to transmit speech across long distances.

DATE 1900
KEY INVENTORS
GUGLIELMO MARCONI

Marconi sent the first radio signal across the Atlantic Ocean in 1901

"THIS VITAL DISCOVERY WOULD LATER DEVELOP THE ABILITY TO TRANSMIT SPEECH"

The Spirit of Invention

Victoria was the first British monarch to be photographed

DATE 1884
KEY INVENTORS
GEORGE EASTMAN

PHOTOGRAPHIC FILM

The Victorians enjoyed taking photographs of their loved ones, whether alive or even post-mortem. The technology quickly developed from the earliest camera in 1826 and Queen Victoria became the first British monarch to have her photograph taken. For a long time it was an expensive and laborious process but one man set out to make the camera "as convenient as the pencil".

American entrepreneur and keen photographer George Eastman invented paper-based photographic film and a roll holder, which made it possible for people to capture candid photos quickly. By 1901 he had founded the Eastman Kodak Company and developed the Kodak Brownie, a camera that everyday people could afford to own. This film helped develop the motion picture industry and it was the first company to produce photography kits for the masses. Kodak still exists today, but sadly it has shifted its focus from cameras to printers.

TELEPHONE

Some of the greatest inventions known to man were made completely by accident and Alexander Graham Bell's breakthrough was no different. While experimenting with electro-audio stimulation, he used two springs connected by a long piece of wire. He gave one end to his assistant, Thomas Watson, and he held the other in a different room.

The idea was that when one spring was moved, the other would too, but actually what happened was that the sound of the spring moving travelled down the wire and was heard at the other end. This device struggled to carry the sound of their voices, but Bell knew he had something, so quickly registered for a patent to stop others from using the same idea. Only two hours after Bell had submitted his request, another inventor had tried to register the same patent but was too late and the fame would forever belong to Bell.

"BELL KNEW HE HAD SOMETHING, SO QUICKLY REGISTERED FOR A PATENT TO STOP OTHERS FROM USING THE SAME IDEA"

DATE 1876
KEY INVENTORS
ALEXANDER GRAHAM BELL

Industry & Invention

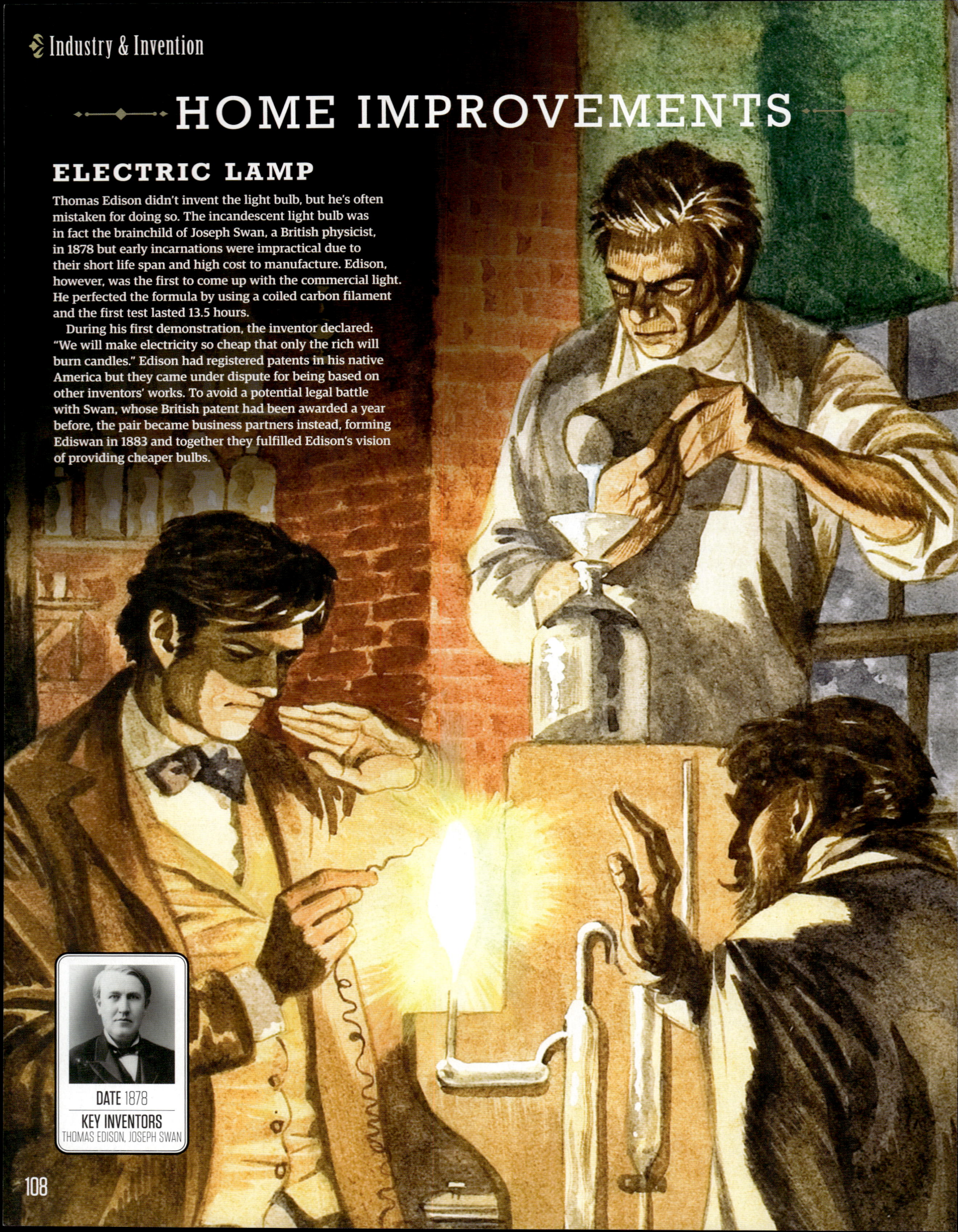

HOME IMPROVEMENTS

ELECTRIC LAMP

Thomas Edison didn't invent the light bulb, but he's often mistaken for doing so. The incandescent light bulb was in fact the brainchild of Joseph Swan, a British physicist, in 1878 but early incarnations were impractical due to their short life span and high cost to manufacture. Edison, however, was the first to come up with the commercial light. He perfected the formula by using a coiled carbon filament and the first test lasted 13.5 hours.

During his first demonstration, the inventor declared: "We will make electricity so cheap that only the rich will burn candles." Edison had registered patents in his native America but they came under dispute for being based on other inventors' works. To avoid a potential legal battle with Swan, whose British patent had been awarded a year before, the pair became business partners instead, forming Ediswan in 1883 and together they fulfilled Edison's vision of providing cheaper bulbs.

DATE 1878
KEY INVENTORS
THOMAS EDISON, JOSEPH SWAN

The Spirit of Invention

VACUUM CLEANER

Hubert Booth's light bulb moment came when he observed an American's new cleaning invention that blew out air. He thought it would be far more efficient if the contraption sucked in air instead and the idea evolved into the vacuum cleaner, a device that almost every household in the modern world couldn't be without. What made Booth believe that he was really onto something was when demonstrating to friends at a posh London restaurant. He placed his handkerchief on the velvet seat of his chair and inhaled as hard as he could, before coughing and spluttering because of all the dust that had come out of the cushion. The handkerchief didn't fare so well either, as Booth and his friends discovered that it was now filthy.

An invention was born, but far from the slender pieces of equipment we have nowadays, this vacuum cleaner was so cumbersome it had to be drawn by a horse and cart. This was because most Victorian houses didn't have electricity so Booth's machine got its power from coal or oil. It would park outside a house and an extra-long hose would snake in through the windows, ridding homes of years and years of accumulated dust.

DATE 1901
KEY INVENTORS HUBERT BOOTH

FLUSHING TOILET SYSTEM

Many inventions are born out of a need to fix a problem and using an earth closet was enough to drive several inventors to work on a solution. This primitive lavatory, or 'privy', was simply a wooden bench with a hole cut out and a bucket underneath, where dry earth was used to cover waste. Naturally, they were pretty whiffy and most privies could be found at the bottom of the garden for this very reason, while chamber pots were used in the house for any night-time emergencies. It was hardly fit for a queen, but Queen Victoria did indeed use an earth closet at Windsor Castle. In 1852, a successful, state-of-the-art loo arrived when pottery manufacturer Thomas Twyford invented the first flushing toilet. It was made of china instead of wood or metal, but the design wasn't entirely original, having been based on the attempts of inventor JG Jennings, yet Twyford was hailed as a pioneer in hygiene.

> "QUEEN VICTORIA DID INDEED USE AN EARTH CLOSET AT WINDSOR CASTLE"

DATE 1852
KEY INVENTORS THOMAS TWYFORD

Industry & Invention

Scheele's Green: The Dye of Death

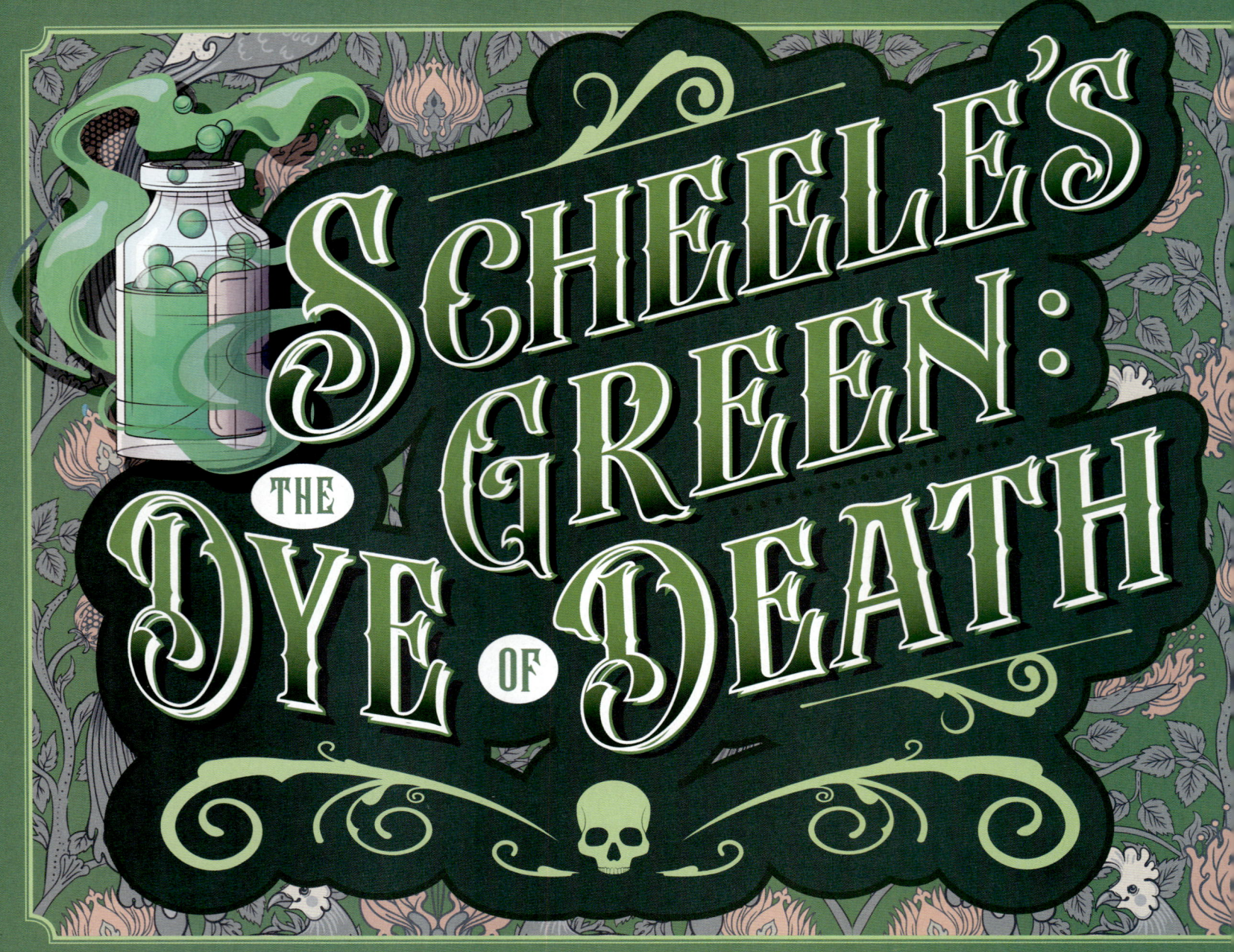

It was the go-to colour of the fashion-conscious Victorian, designed to bring nature into the drawing room, but it also brought death

Written by Dr Joanna Elphick

Thanks to the Industrial Revolution, the Victorian landscape was overshadowed by clouds of black soot and grey smoke. The public craved nature and people wanted to bring the natural world inside their homes. The easiest way was to paint the walls in vivid hues and none was more in demand than green, particularly Scheele's Green.

Invented in 1775 by Carl Wilhelm Scheele, Scheele's Green was an instant success. The pigment was used in paint, wallpaper, bookbindings, clothing, faux flowers, and as a food dye. Greenock's green blancmange was eagerly gobbled up by children in the nursery whilst their mother burnt Scheele's Green candles in her elegant green drawing room and their father stepped out in his finest green waistcoat. William Morris, the celebrated designer, led the way in creating floral wallpaper. His green *Daisy* wallpaper design of 1864 was an instant success and even Buckingham Palace famously adorned the walls with Scheele's Green-coloured wallpaper.

This vibrant and extremely profitable colour was different to any other dye on the market and therefore highly sought after, but the must-have home hue came at a price far beyond mere pennies and pounds for it also cost lives.

Inventor Scheele developed the colourant by heating sodium carbonate, adding arsenious oxide, followed by copper sulphate, and mixing until the solution was dissolved. It made a beautiful dye, but it also created a toxic timebomb. Poisonous particles were being released throughout fashionable Victorian homes, whilst damp, moldy wallpaper released arsine gases into the air.

Unbeknownst to Scheele, his fabulous dye was poisoning the nation. Nausea,

Scheele's Green: The Dye of Death

Proud parents dressed their children from head to foot in the latest green styles, unaware that the dyed cloth rubbing against their skin was highly toxic

Queen Victoria's private chapel at Buckingham Palace was decorated with arsenic-laced faux flowers that had been delicately painted with Scheele's Green dye

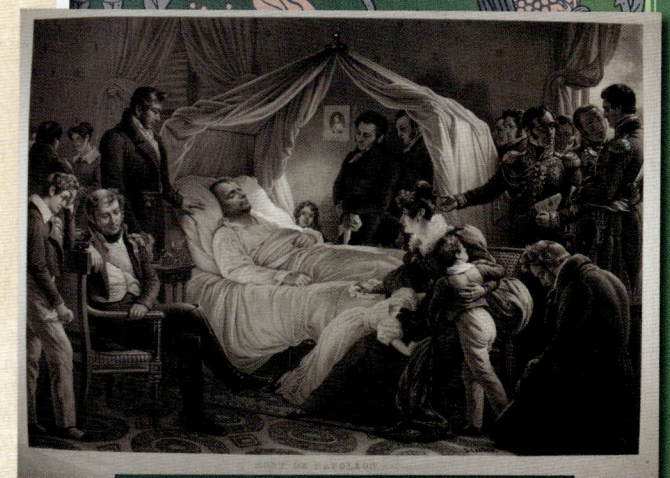

As the dye is a carcinogenic, it's thought that Napoleon's stomach cancer may have been induced by the green walls of his St Helena home

vomiting, diarrhea and agonising abdominal cramps were often accompanied by hallucinations. Combined with their unhealthy preoccupation with death and the supernatural, many individuals firmly believed they were being regularly visited by paranormal entities who, it seemed, were particularly attracted to the freshly wallpapered parlours.

In 1858, 21 people died from eating green sweeties, meanwhile adults were becoming nauseous after imbibing green-tinged beverages. Children that had been employed to dust faux flowers with arsenic-laced dye, were covered in open sores and when one young flower maker, Matilda Scheurer, died from exposure to the poison in 1861, the public began to fear the colour that they had previously clamoured for. Clearly the dye wasn't worth dying for. Public pressure to ban the colour peaked after Queen Victoria ordered that her Scheele's Green paper be stripped from the Palace's walls and it quickly fell out of fashion.

> "MANY PEOPLE BELIEVED THEY WERE BEING VISITED BY PARANORMAL ENTITIES WHO WERE PARTICULARLY ATTRACTED TO FRESHLY WALLPAPERED PARLOURS"

Industry & Invention

Twilight Sleep

The first anaesthetics for childbirth were used in the Victorian era, but each had their own issues and shortcomings

Written by Jack Griffiths

Giving birth during the Victorian era was painful and dangerous. Mothers died in around one in every 200 births across the period. It wasn't until the 1850s that anaesthetics were routinely trialled to help relieve the pain. And each one had fluctuating results.

The first local anaesthetics to be used were nitrous oxide (laughing gas) and ether. However both had issues with efficiency and were replaced by morphine and chloroform. The state in which these anaesthetics would leave mothers was known as Dämmerschlaf or Twilight Sleep. This involved an injection of morphine and scopolamine that would both reduce the pain of childbirth and put the mother to sleep with little or no recollection of the birth of her child. Often, it would also take place in a dark room where she would have a covering over her eyes and ears and be strapped down to further restrain her. This procedure was particularly popular in Germany in the early 20th century but its safety and humanity was questioned, as well as the frequent side-effects of delirium and slowed breathing. There were also negative post-procedure effects of Twilight Sleep. The cocktail of drugs could be passed onto the baby, which could affect their breathing, and the mother being unconscious meant there was no opportunity for mother and baby to bond. Mothers would wake after the birth in a state of drowsy confusion, mentally affecting both them and the baby.

The use of chloroform as an anaesthetic was first pioneered by Sir James Young Simpson in 1847. It went on to be used as a pain relief in both surgery and childbirth and was endorsed by no other than Queen Victoria herself when she gave birth to her eighth child in 1853. Prince Leopold was delivered after the queen held a cloth soaked in chloroform to her face to numb the pain. She would use it again when giving birth to Princess Beatrice four years later. The use of chloroform increased after this royal seal of approval but its rise was curtailed. The chemical had detractors from the start and it was twice denied usage for previous royal pregnancies after evidence of its toxic qualities and its usage resulting in medical complications.

The use of morphine, scopolamine and chloroform as an anaesthetic in labour declined in the early 20th century as other safer and more effective anaesthetics were sought out.

Twilight Sleep

Pain relief was only accessible to the few who could afford it, including Queen Victoria who gave chloroform the royal seal of approval

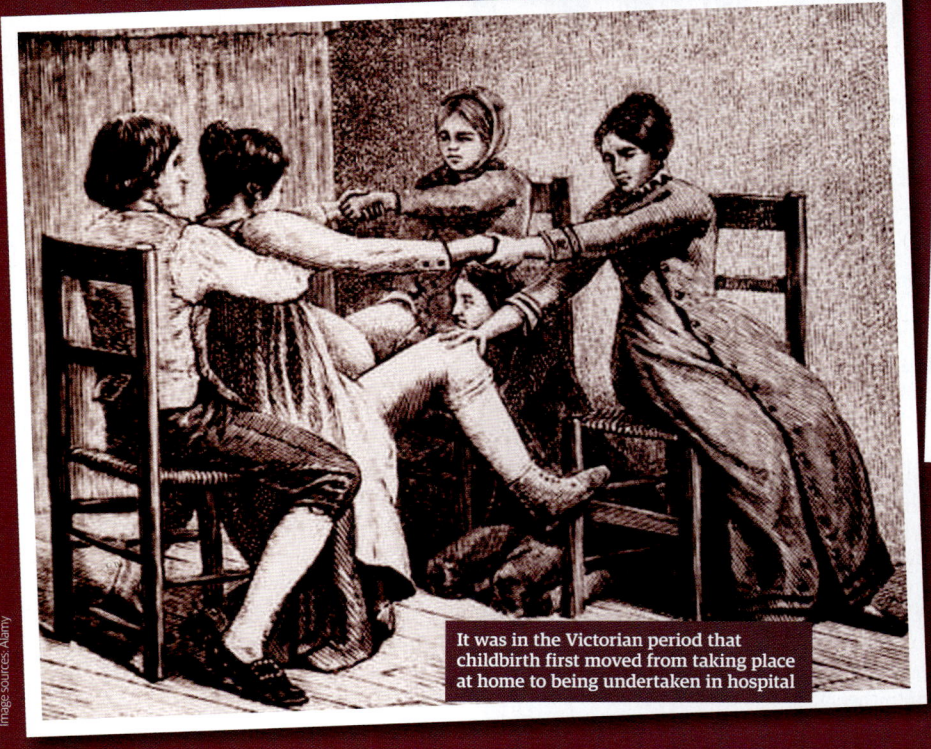

As the popularity of Twilight Sleep increased, so did errors in drug administration, causing too much or too little sleep induction and pain relief

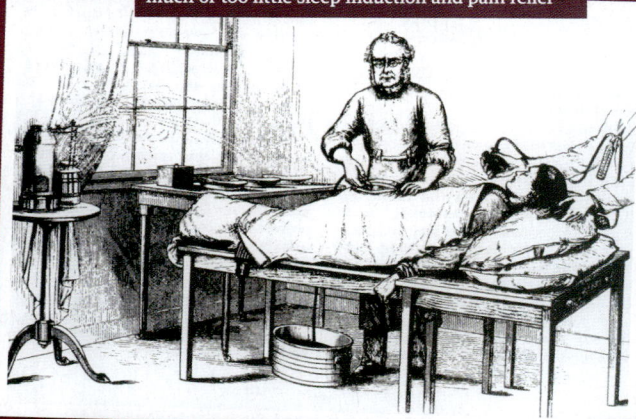

It was in the Victorian period that childbirth first moved from taking place at home to being undertaken in hospital

> "TWILIGHT SLEEP INVOLVED AN INJECTION OF MORPHINE AND SCOPOLAMINE"

113

Industry & Invention

THE EYE OF THE BEHOLDER

We live in a world of Botox and injectables, but Victorian beauty standards might make even the most needle-happy modern fashionista shudder

Written by Catherine Curzon

> Belladonna, also known as deadly nightshade, was used in eyedrops to give fashionable, dewy eyes. It also caused inoperable blindness

Victorian fashion and beauty was big business and for women who could afford to follow the most modern fashions, it cost big money too. As they stepped out into polite society and lit up the ballrooms of one of history's most glittering eras, Victorian women used their wardrobes and their make-up bags as social weapons. Status, gentility and taste could be suggested by something as subtle as pale skin or the biggest bustle, and they would stop at nothing to achieve the idea. From corsetry and bustles to belladonna eye drops and a diet that relied on hungry tapeworms, the Victorians did nothing by halves.

UNDERPINNINGS

For some people, underwear has always been a serious business and in the 19th century, it was as vital to the success of a stylish look as foundations were vital to the successful construction of a building. Get the underpinnings wrong and nothing that went on top would sit as it should.

Victorian ladies of fashion sought to achieve the perfect shape for their era, which dictated that they should have a narrow waist and wide hips, accentuated by layers of expensive petticoats and finally, an expensive frock to finish the look. For this, they relied on dramatic underpinnings that completely reshaped their silhouette. The shape and fit of the corset had been developing over generations to arrive at the famed and instantly

The Eye Of The Beholder

DR MACKENZIE'S ARSENICAL SOAP

Prepared with Arsenic, Zinc, and other Ingredients. As a beautifier of the skin and complexion.

6d. & 1/- per tablet

MADAME PATTI says :— " Most Excellent."

Eradicates Spots and all Imperfections

Of all Chemists, &c., or post free from

HARVEY, Ltd., 5, Denman Street, London Bridge, S.E,

In the Victorian era, arsenic soap, face cream and more was a decidedly deadly way to achieve perfect, pale skin

recognisable Victorian model, often the corset that springs to mind when a casual observer imagines the garment. Something else that springs to mind is a tightly-laced, agonisingly constricted waist, but this was not the norm. In fact, it was far from it.

Whilst some women practised tightlacing - the common misconception is that it was something that every woman did, a myth further enhanced by the mistaken belief that some women even had ribs removed to narrow their waists to an extreme degree - neither of these beliefs has any basis in fact. Instead, the vast majority of women wore their corsets laced to a comfortable tightness that would still give them the desired narrow waist and accentuated hips, but without the discomfort and breathlessness associated with tightlacing. Rib removal, meanwhile, is simply a myth.

BUSTLING ABOUT

Those fashionably accentuated hips were helped initially by crinoline wire frames that sometimes expanded to an eye-popping radius and were worn under layers of skirt and petticoat to create a bell shape. Made out of metal and later horsehair and whalebone, the crinoline was the height of fashion for a time, hidden beneath elaborate hoop skirts.

As fashion moved on, the popularity of the crinoline began to decline and by the late 1870s its era had ended. Instead, fashionable women had fallen in love with the bustle, which caused the back of a gown to push out at the waist. The bustle was born out of the crinoline, which grew flatter in the front over the years, until it turned into a crinolette, which had hoops only at the back whilst flat at the front. Uncomfortable to wear and difficult for sitting, the crinolette didn't last.

The bustle was the natural evolution from this. It sat over the bottom and was tied around the waist. Constructed from a frame of metal padded with wool, horsehair or another substance, the bustle later developed into a wire cage that sat like a shelf at the rump, with the skirt's fabric draped over it. By the 1880s, collapsible bustles had been developed, which collapsed to allow the wearer to sit.

The bustle fell out of fashion in the late 1870s, before returning with a vengeance a couple of years later. It eventually survived into the 1910s, before women turned their backs on such extravagant underpinnings and fashion strode into a new era.

COSMETIC CALAMITIES

In the Georgian era, the attitude to make up often seemed like the more the merrier. White faces, rouged lips and beauty marks were the hallmarks of high Georgian excess in all its splendour. However, the Regency era saw such painting fall out of fashion in favour of a pale-skinned, unadorned naturalism that encouraged an almost invisible make-up palette. This was the look that the Victorians embraced too, and it was certainly

With her narrow waist and accentuated rear, this Victorian lady's dramatic bustle and exaggerated corset make her the height of fashion

115

Industry & Invention

the approach that the young Queen Victoria took in her own use of cosmetics.

In Victorian Britain, heavy make-up was a sure sign of moral turpitude. It was worn by sex workers or actresses, two groups that ladies in polite society had no wish to be associated with. When it came to achieving a perfect Victorian beauty, however, fashionable women might have been averse to heavy rouge, but they didn't mind employing what could prove to be fatal tricks.

ARSENIC EVERYTHING

Whilst Georgian women painted deadly lead-based paints on their skin, Victorians put their trust in the equally dangerous poison, arsenic. Arsenic was a miracle of the age, lending a vivid green to everything from wallpaper to clothing and, in the early years of the queen's reign, arsenic green dresses were enormously popular.

Although crinolines, petticoats, shifts and corsets meant much of the dress didn't make contact with the skin, where it did the results could be horrendous. Open sores and ulcers began to erupt on the wearer's skin and as she sweated, more arsenic seeped from the dye and into her pores. In extreme cases, women experienced blindness, hair loss and eventually organ failure and death. The dye continued to be used though, with the true casualties being the women who produced it en masse. Their lives were cut horribly short by continued exposure to the poison and they died as a result of arsenic poisoning.

ARSENIC EATERS

It wasn't only clothes that exposed fashionable Victorians to arsenic either. The poison was believed to cause sparkling eyes and a translucent complexion, free of blemishes and imperfections (as well as ulcers, poisoning and death, of course) and women nibbled on arsenic wafers in the hope of achieving these results. There was no conspiracy to hide the poison either; many of the products stated it proudly in names such as Dr Simm's Arsenic Complexion Wafers, or Dr Mackenzie's Arsenical Soap.

Paleness was the fashion and arsenic soaps, skin creams and wafers provided exactly that. That they did it by killing red blood cells was, of course, not mentioned in the adverts. To the contrary, Dr Mackenzie struck again with their Improved Harmless Arsenic Complexion Wafers. Unsurprisingly, they were anything but the harmless beauty supplement they claimed to be.

BRIGHT, SIGHTLESS EYES

Throughout history, tuberculosis - also known as consumption - was a feared and fatal illness. The consumptive look, however, with pale skin and dilated, dewy eyes, was seen as a beauty ideal. In order to achieve those dewy eyes, women used eyedrops containing belladonna - otherwise known as deadly nightshade, the infamously poisonous plant.

Used in high doses or for a prolonged period, the result was blindness. For those who couldn't afford belladonna drops, lemon or orange juice was squirted directly onto the eyeball. It achieved a watery look, naturally, whilst being intensely painful. At least it wouldn't blind you, though.

MERCURIAL LASHES

A face wash utilising a cocktail of ammonia, mercury and opium was the perfect night-time regime for some who sought the fashionable pale look, especially when it was followed on waking by a refreshing wash with yet more ammonia first thing in the morning. Mercury was also used around the eyes to encourage the growth of desirable eyelashes, whilst slowly poisoning you.

DROP DEAD GORGEOUS

It goes without saying that none of these Victorian beauty regimes are recommended in the modern age. With blindness, maiming and death very real side effects of the search for the Victorian beauty ideal, such practices have long since been consigned to history. Next time you see an image of a picture-perfect Victorian lady, silk-clad and stunning in her corset and bustle, her face flawless and her eyes bright, just remember what it might have cost her to get there. As the 19th-century French saying goes, "beauty is pain", and nobody could attest to that better than the Victorians.

> "IN VICTORIAN BRITAIN, HEAVY MAKE-UP WAS A SURE SIGN OF MORAL TURPITUDE"

A bracing facewash of ammonia or mercury was a popular Victorian beauty trick. Needless to say, don't try this at home

---

THE TAPEWORM DIET
Why starve yourself when popping a parasite can do the job?

When Victorians wanted to drop a few pounds, there was one method that has led to hot debate amongst historians: the tapeworm diet.

It sounds simple enough, the dieter simply swallows a pill containing a tapeworm egg. Once the egg hatches, the tapeworm latches on to its host and gets busy ingesting a little of everything the patient eats. As the tapeworm grows, so the patient loses ever more weight yet never feels hungry.

The problem, however, is that there is no way to tell the tapeworm to stop. Once the patient reached their desired weight, the worm had to be removed and that was far from simple. Some used specially adapted tubes containing food, which doctors lowered down their throats to tempt the parasite out. Another solution was for the dieter to sit with their mouth open in front of a bowl of milk until the tapeworm slithered its way out.

Take heart in the fact that some historians claim that this diet was nothing more than a placebo and that the pills had no tapeworm egg inside them at all. The people who purchased them truly believed in their powers though, so desperate to achieve a fashionable ideal that a hitchhiking tapeworm seemed like a small price to pay.

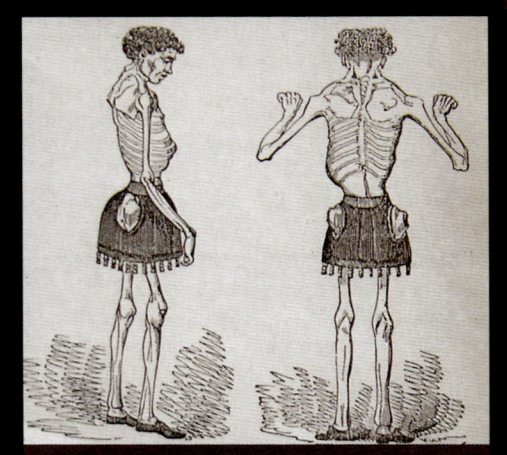

Claude-Ambroise 'The Human Skeleton' Seurat was a freakshow exhibit in the 19th century. His physique was attributed to a five-metre-long tapeworm

The Eye Of The Beholder

Empress Elisabeth of Austria, known as Sisi, was one woman who really did love to tightlace her corsets, achieving a waist of 16 inches

117

Industry & Invention

THE GOLDEN AGE OF TAXIDERMY

How the pickling, skinning, stuffing and preserving of dead animals went from esoteric ancient Egyptian practice, to the height of Victorian fashion and a royal collection

Written by Ben Biggs

At its Victorian peak, Britain had tendrils that stretched from a small island nation in the northern Atlantic, around the world to colonies on every continent. The Empire wielded staggering power and influence, while the most affluent Britons were truly rolling in money: they sought to furnish their stately homes and estates with ostentatious symbols of their wealth and cultivation. They were avid collectors of antiques and objets d'art, especially curios from far-flung cultures. So when John Hancock's *Struggle with the Quarry* - a glass cage containing a stuffed eel slipping out of the grasp of a stuffed heron being attacked by a stuffed gyrafalcon - was displayed at the 1851 Crystal Palace Great Exhibition in London, it lit a fire under the feet of Victorian dilettantes. Suddenly, anyone who was anyone with enough cash to flash wanted stuffed animals in their collection - the more exotic, the better.

Hancock's piece was the most lifelike and dynamic of taxidermy specimens at the 1851 exhibition, but it was far from the only one. The headliner was an elephant that had been requisitioned from a local museum for the Indian display. It was the thick hide of the unfortunate animal stretched over a frame, moreover it was an African elephant skin, but even if anyone could tell the difference, no-one seemed to care. In an era when photography was still in its infancy, this was the first time that some were seeing this majestic creature, let alone getting close to one.

After this, even Queen Victoria wanted in, using her reach as arguably the most powerful person in the world to amass a considerable collection of stuffed birds. Taxidermists, often with signature techniques for preserving and creating the most lifelike displays, sprung out of the woodwork offering their services to those that could afford them. Organs were carefully removed through orifices so as not to tear or damage the skin in any way, after which a toxic arsenic solution was used to stave off the natural process of decay. To survive a long, overseas journey intact, whole animals were pickled in barrels or their skins cured in alum salts to dry them out, rather like a side of gravadlax (try not to imagine it, you'll never eat salmon again). A coating of turpentine was often used to keep the flies away. This nauseating process was done in the name of science and art although, ethics aside, macabre Victorian taxidermy like Nicholay and Son's Great Exhibition display (see picture) might turn the stomach of modern artists and conservationists alike.

The Golden Age of Taxidermy

Furs and exotic stuffed animals heaped upon each other in Nicholay and Son's 1851 Great Exhibition display

There was good money to be made in stuffing and preserving animals for the most renowned Victorian taxidermists

UNRIVALLED EXHIBITION HONOURS.
TY-TWO GOLD, SILVER, & BRONZE MEDALS, DIPLOMAS OF HONOUR.

and Special Prizes including the
LEADING PRIZE FOR BEST SPECIMENS OF TAXIDERMY,
were awarded at the Great International Fisheries Exhibition, London, 1883, to

T. E. GUNN,
Naturalist,
PRESERVER OF ANIMALS, BIRDS, REPTILES, FISH, &c.,
84, & 86 ST. GILES' STREET, NORWICH.
Also awarded upwards of Forty First-Class Prizes (including five Gold Medals) Special Silver Cups and Silver Medals at National Exhibitions.

An 'Indian' elephant with howdah at the 1851 Great Exhibition. The elephant had been shot in South Africa and was already being displayed in a local museum

119

Industry & Invention

CSI: WHITECHAPEL

When the Met Police were called on to find Jack the Ripper, would the newest forensic techniques help them?

Written by Nell Darby

When a ruthless killer struck in the heart of East London in the autumn of 1888, there was ample opportunity for the capital's policemen and detectives to employ a range of forensic science methods to help them catch a killer. The subsequent crime investigations, had they used these new techniques, might have been more successful than they ultimately proved to be.

The first woman now regarded to be one of the 'canonical five' victims of Jack the Ripper was Mary Ann Nichols, who was found dead in the early hours of 31 August 1888 in Buck's Row, Whitechapel. The police investigation started with traditional methods, questioning those in the neighbourhood - in particular, the local prostitutes who worked the streets there.

Nine days later, at 6am on 8 September, a second woman was found in the backyard of 29 Hanbury Street - Annie Chapman. On 30 September, Elizabeth Stride was found in Berner Street, and less than an hour later Catherine Eddowes was found dead. Prior to Catherine's murder, all the killings had taken place in parts of East London that came under the jurisdiction of the Metropolitan Police; Eddowes, however, was found in Mitre Square, part of the Square Mile, and so the Met was now joined by officers from the City of London Police in their investigations.

It was reported that after killing Catherine Eddowes, the alleged murderer had walked from Mitre Square to Goulstone Street, where he had thrown away a piece of Catherine's apron, on which he had wiped the blood from his hands and knife. Nearby, he had written on a wall, 'The Jews are the men that will not be blamed for nothing'. On 1 October, the police revealed that the Central News Agency had been sent a letter the previous week purporting to be from the murderer. It was addressed 'Dear Boss' and signed 'Jack the Ripper' - a name that caught the public imagination. Now, a link was made between the writing in this letter, and that of the graffiti, with the press

> "The police investigation started with traditional methods, questioning those in the neighbourhood"

The police find a victim of Jack the Ripper, lying openly in the street

FORENSIC PIONEERS

The founding fathers of crime scene investigation

Francis Galton
Specialism: Fingerprinting
This British scientist brought scientific rigour to the analysis of fingerprints, after he produced a study of their uniqueness in 1888. Galton also created the first fingerprint classification system, which would provide the basis for the system introduced by Scotland Yard in 1901 and swiftly rolled out across the English-speaking world.

Alphonse Bertillon
Specialism: Mugshots
This French police officer standardised how mugshots were taken, so that they always included a front view of the face and both side views. He also introduced a system of measurements to better record suspect's physical features. The Paris Police Prefecture first used Bertillion's methods in 1882 and by 1887 it was being used as far afield as Illinois.

Mathieu Orfila
Specialism: Toxicology
Often called the 'Father of Toxicology,' this Spanish-born chemist was an early pioneer in the field of identifying poisons. In 1814, he wrote his *Treatise On Poisons*, and he was regularly called on to give evidence in trials, most notably in the 1840 murder trial of Marie Lafarge. Orfila also researched asphyxiation, the decomposition of bodies, and exhumation.

Bernard Spilsbury
Specialism: Pathology
Britain's most celebrity CSI, Sir Bernard became a career expert witness after his forensic evidence convicted Dr Hawley Crippen for killing his showgirl wife, in a case that captivated Edwardian England. While he was a hard-working pathologist, believed to have completed around 20,000 autopsies, new research suggests his fame may have wrongly swayed both judges and juries, leading to several miscarriages of justice.

Edmond Locard
Specialism: Clothing analysis
The so-called 'Sherlock Holmes of France' wrote a seven-volume series, *Treaty Of Criminalistics*, that argued whenever two surfaces touched, something would be transferred from one to the other – fibres, paint, blood, and so on. Therefore, as part of this 'exchange principle', the microscopic examination of clothing could reveal minute pieces of evidence.

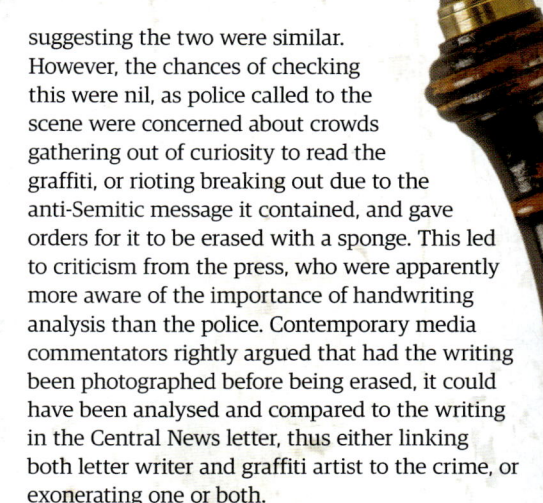

suggesting the two were similar. However, the chances of checking this were nil, as police called to the scene were concerned about crowds gathering out of curiosity to read the graffiti, or rioting breaking out due to the anti-Semitic message it contained, and gave orders for it to be erased with a sponge. This led to criticism from the press, who were apparently more aware of the importance of handwriting analysis than the police. Contemporary media commentators rightly argued that had the writing been photographed before being erased, it could have been analysed and compared to the writing in the Central News letter, thus either linking both letter writer and graffiti artist to the crime, or exonerating one or both.

The Metropolitan Police has since been excused for some of its perceived failings on the grounds that forensic science was not, at the time, an

121

Industry & Invention

THE SCENE OF A CRIME

The killing ground can contain many types of forensic evidence

01 Forensic footwear evidence
Footwear and footprint analysis is a form of forensics that was used by Sherlock Holmes in two of his cases *A Study In Scarlet* (1887) and *The Sign Of The Four* (1890), and he noted that "there is no branch of detective science which is so important". Footwear impressions can tell investigators the number of people at a crime scene, the type of footwear, and even the wearer's approximate height. Widely used today, the study of footwear was initially slow to take off.

02 Handwriting analysis
The subject of graphology – the study of handwriting – had interested philosophers since the 17th century, but it was in the 1870s that Frenchman Jean Michon published his research into handwriting analysis. In 1871, Rosa Baugham did the same, and the *Strand* magazine similarly published articles on the subject. From the 1890s, as psychology developed as a profession, the area started to attract considerable research. Handwriting analysis involves looking at shapes and patterns in writing to see how they reflect the writer's personality.

03 Poisons and toxicology
Toxicology is 'the science of poisons'. Poisoning, particularly by arsenic, was a common way to murder someone in the 19th century as for a long time arsenic went undetected inside the body. However, by the 1850s, post-mortems could find arsenic grains in murder victims' stomachs. In 1888, a military surgeon, Philip Eustace Cross, was hanged in Cork for murdering his wife, Mary. The crime was detected only after Mary's body was exhumed, and an examination showed symptoms of arsenic poisoning.

04 Bullet matching
Back in 1835, the Metropolitan Police located the purchaser of a bullet by looking at flaws in that bullet and then finding the mould used to make it. It was also found that tiny marks or flaws in bullets could help locate the gun barrel those bullets had come from. But it was still difficult to confirm these facts, though, and it was not until 1926 that bullet matching could be used as evidence in court trials.

08 Forensic odontology
It's a grand name, but it simply refers to the analysis of bite marks and dental remains. The use of bite marks in trial evidence dates back to late 17th century United States, but the first use of bite mark evidence to convict a criminal in England occurred in 1906. In this case, the offender, a burglar, had left a bite mark in a piece of cheese at the crime scene; his teeth were found to 'fit' the mark.

"Other victims had been found outside and police had been keen to remove their bodies as soon as possible"

CSI: Whitechapel

05 Clothing analysis
The analysis of clothing or footwear can reveal fibres transferred from one individual to another, evidence of a change in location – for example, looking at mud or other substances in the tread of footwear – and even traces of blood, saliva or semen that can help identify either a victim or a suspect. This type of analysis was popularised by Edmond Locard in France, but it has since become a fundamental part of the forensic scientist's work.

06 Fingerprint analysis
In 1892, the first ever fingerprint bureau opened in Argentina after a notorious murder case where the murderer was identified by a bloody fingerprint. Sir William Herschel used fingerprints to identify individuals in India, but in the UK, Francis Galton was at the forefront of fingerprint analysis. In the Edwardian era, one man convicted of burglary following successful fingerprint analysis was William Brown, who robbed a shop in Poplar, East London, but had left his prints on a window.

07 Blood type
Given that blood can so often be left at a crime scene, it is not surprising that it a valuable form of evidence. In the 1860s, spectrum analysis was used to locate bloodstains, and other processes were developed in the 1880s. In 1900, the blood groups – A, B and O – were identified and so led the way for blood type analysis, whereby blood left at a scene could be identified as a victim's – or the suspect's.

'integral' part of criminal investigation, and that scientific evidence was not recognised as an important part of criminal investigations until the 1890s.

However, the Met did use photographs of victims and crime scenes as part of its investigation, although these crime scene photographs were not done as we would today, or for the same reasons. Whereas today they record the scene, the victim, and potential evidence or clues, during the Whitechapel murders, photographs of the victims' eyes were said to have been taken. This was due to the mistaken belief that a dying person's eyes would record the final image they had seen. Therefore, it was hoped that the Ripper victims' eyes might preserve an image of the murderer, caught in the act of killing. Although this sounds absurd to us today, the Victorian era was a curious mix of modernity and superstition, and as with other cases during the 19th century, the Jack the Ripper investigation combined modern techniques with the traditional, and even the supernatural.

Surviving photographs from the time include mortuary photographs of four victims, as well as images of the final victim Mary Jane Kelly's body in her bed. Other victims had been found outside, in the East London streets, and police had been keen to move their bodies as soon as possible to prevent onlookers gawping or panic setting in - although drawings were made of where Catherine Eddowes was murdered.

In Mary Jane Kelly's case, however, she was murdered in her lodgings at 13 Miller's Court, in Spitalfields, on the night of 8 November. Her body could be left where it was as it was indoors, away from prying eyes. However, the infamous image of Kelly's mutilated body in situ only came into existence thanks to the failure of another method of forensic examination.

Although police were called upon Mary Jane's body being discovered, they loitered outside her lodgings for some time, rather than going straight in. Inspector Frederick Abberline, a Scotland Yard man who had been seconded to H Division in Whitechapel after Mary Ann Nichols's murder, believed bloodhounds had been sent for and did not want officers to contaminate the crime scene until after the dogs had been.

However, as time passed and the dogs still had not appeared, Inspector Abberline decided to start without them. Reasoning one man entering the lodging was better than a large group, a local photographer was sent for and told to take pictures of the body as it lay on the bed.

Even when it became apparent two hours later that the sniffer dogs would not be coming, the police instigated a more forensically advanced plan than with previous victims. In such a horrific scene as Mary Jane Kelly's room, Abberline concluded there must be some clues preserved somewhere, and that these merited a proper crime scene investigation. They therefore left her body on the bed while they carried out a full, in-depth,

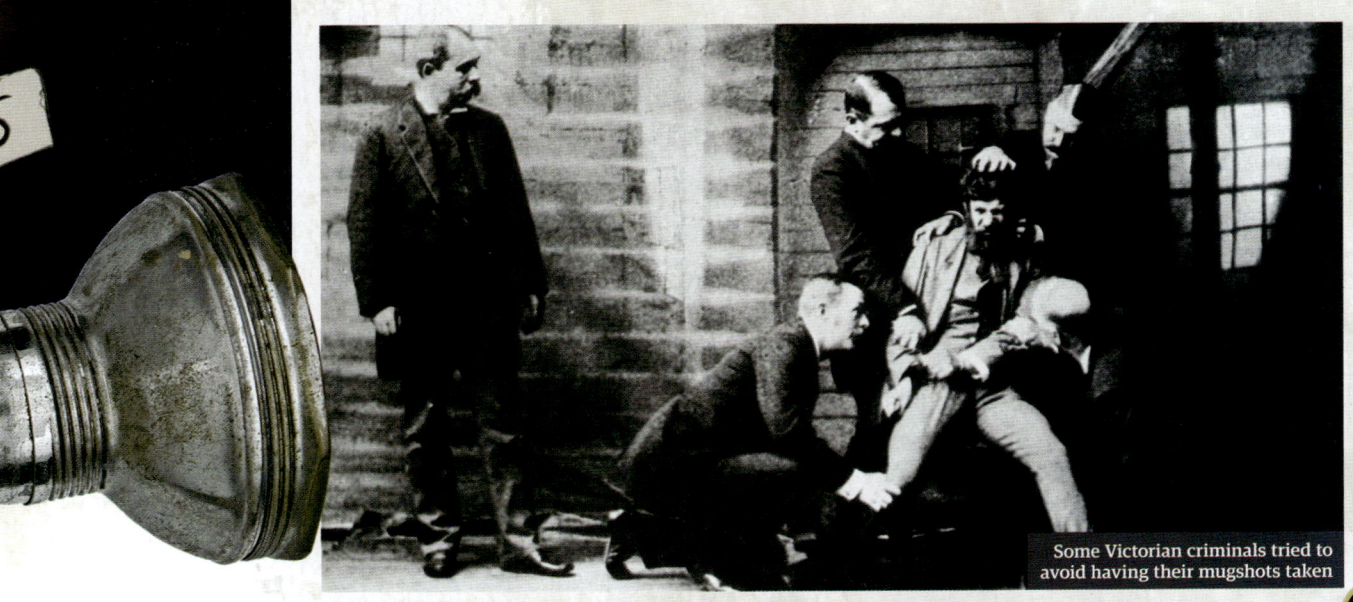

The 'Dear Boss' letter: what could handwriting analysis reveal?

Some Victorian criminals tried to avoid having their mugshots taken

Industry & Invention

examination of the poverty-stricken woman's rooms. Unfortunately, the inspector was forced to report that "nothing [was found] of any assistance to us".

Abberline's assumption that bloodhounds might be called in was not a fanciful one. Sniffer dogs had already been used elsewhere, for centuries, in order to find missing people and animals. Met Police Commissioner Sir Charles Warren, under pressure to catch the killer, debated the use of hounds, wondering whether dogs would be able to track a scent if the killer left any clothing or blood behind, or whether an outdoor, urban crime scene would involve so many passers-by that the dogs would be confused. To find out more, in the early morning of Tuesday 9 October 1888, Sir Charles arrived in Regent's Park to watch a group of bloodhounds at work, to see what they could do.

The dogs were owned by Yorkshireman Edwin Brough, who had spent a considerable amount of time both breeding and training his hounds. He had got in touch with the Metropolitan Police nearly a week before Kelly's murder to highlight the use of bloodhounds in tracking criminals, and the police arranged for him to come down to London with two of his dogs - Champion Barnaby and Burgho. Prior to Sir Charles visiting, Brough practised twice with his dogs - once in Regent's Park the morning before, and once in Hyde Park that evening. Both times, the dogs were successful in tracking a young man who was given a 15-minute start, despite the first occasion being frosty and the second dark. When the dogs were made to track more individuals at 7am on Tuesday morning, they again proved a success. Six runs were made in all, with Sir Charles himself gamely acting as the hunted man on two occasions. They proved that they could track down a stranger they had not met before, and Sir Charles, although he didn't express an opinion publicly at the park, seemed pleased with the result.

Police were ordered not to remove the next victim's body, but to instead send word to a named vet who owned several bloodhounds and would be taken to the crime scene to immediately put his dogs onto the scent.

Of course, this all depended on the next victim - and it seemed to be assumed that there would be another victim - being found in circumstances that lent themselves to the use of dogs.

In the event, however, hounds were not used - although Burgho and Barnaby had been shown to have skills, the police were concerned about spending money on these relatively inexperienced dogs. When the Met failed to either buy or hire the dogs, their owner left London with them. Unfortunately, though, as Abberline's confusion showed, not everyone was told that the bloodhounds were no longer available.

The police of the time lacked much of today's knowledge and techniques, but they did try and work with what they could. When Elizabeth Stride's body was discovered, police examined locals' hands and clothing to try and find bloodstains. They searched the walls near to where the body had been found in case they could find blood from the murderer on it, but again had no luck.

Although DNA testing was not in existence then, they knew the importance of finding blood and matching it to a victim, or conversely, ruling it out and suggesting that it might come from a suspect instead. However, they were hampered at various scenes by onlookers crowding round and potentially damaging the crime sites; for example, when Mary Ann Nichols's body still lay on the ground, the doctor who attended was startled by the number of ghoulish onlookers and ordered the body to be removed and taken to the mortuary to be examined, thus perhaps rushing the examination of the crime scene in order to preserve the dead woman's modesty and privacy. The police also claimed to have been hampered by the inefficiency of others - for example, despite the police allegedly giving instructions that Nichols's body was not to be removed again until a full post-mortem had been carried out, two men went and stripped her body, and washed it down (and potentially removing evidence), and getting rid of her clothing. A lack of organisation from some parties may have restricted the chances of finding a killer, even though there was clearly knowledge of where evidence could be found and what techniques might help in finding it.

This illustration of Jack the Ripper owes much to Sherlock Holmes

> "Scotland Yard opened its own fingerprint department in 1901, too late for the Ripper victims"

Those investigating early 20th-century crime scenes employed new scientific methods

The relatively new Criminal Investigation Department of the Metropolitan Police was, inevitably, hampered by the fact that some forensic techniques were still in their infancy and other methods had not yet been invented.

There was certainly blood, but not, apparently, bloody footprints, although the presence of onlookers at some of the crime scenes may have made it impossible to even try and obtain prints.

In addition, at that time, not only was there no DNA testing, but it was not possible to distinguish between animal and human blood – hence the concern at what kind of blood trail hounds would follow. Fingerprinting was about to take off, with the 1890s seeing individuals develop classification systems that recognised the uniqueness of fingerprints – and a careful study of both outdoor and indoor crime scenes in East London might have located fingerprints that came from someone other than the victim. Scotland Yard opened its own fingerprint department in 1901, too late for the Ripper victims.

In other respects, though, reports do not suggest that other techniques were considered, even when they existed at the time. For example, Sir Arthur Conan Doyle had written about the value of footprint analysis the year before the murders in *A Study In Scarlet*, but there is no mention of footprints – either their presence or absence – in the press.

Anthropometrics, the identification of criminals by their appearance, which could have helped to rule in or rule out any suspects, had been invented in the 1880s, but Scotland Yard only started to use it years after the murders took place.

In investigating Jack the Ripper, the police tried to use a mix of old and new techniques with little success. If they had been able to use all the forensic methods being developed over the late 19th and early 20th century, perhaps they might have had more luck and we would have the answer to who Jack the Ripper actually was.

The Police News front page reports the deaths of Elizabeth Stride and Catharine Eddowes

Sherlock Holmes (seen here portrayed by Basil Rathbone) may have been fictional, but he utilised many real forensic techniques

SHERLOCK HOLMES, FORENSIC SCIENTIST

Fictional detective Sherlock Holmes once stated to his friend Watson that, "Detection is, or ought to be, an exact science", and from his first appearance in print in 1887, his methods were as scientific as possible for the era.

Holmes was a truly modern detective: his work both reflected developments in Victorian crime detection, and heralded today's era of scrupulous and methodical forensic science techniques. Sir Arthur Conan Doyle incorporated the latest developments in criminal science into his creation, and even, in some cases, pre-empted them.

Holmes even had his own chemistry lab, where he could spend hours studying and conducting experiments. The Holmes stories also show him using techniques such as footprint analysis, graphology, toxicology (working out in *A Study In Scarlet* that a man has been poisoned with arsenic), and even using a sniffer dog – anthropometrics, fingerprint analysis, and ballistics all get a mention, too. Sherlock Holmes was, then, a forensic scientist at heart, using criminal investigation tactics far before his time – and long before even the police did.

Industry & Invention

The Everlasting Staircase

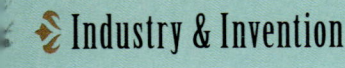

It was designed to instill the 'habits of industry' in the growing number of offenders, but more often than not, it merely broke their spirits

Written by Dr Joanna Elphick

'Idle hands make work for the Devil', or so the saying goes, and the Victorians were quick to link a lack of industrious endeavours with the criminal mind. Nowhere was this more evident than in the prisons where criminals were left to languish. Something was required to occupy their bodies whilst the soul was busy repenting. To this end, Sir William Cubitt invented the penal treadmill in 1817 and the first example of this new punishment was installed in the prisons at Bury St Edmunds and Brixton the following year. Previous miniature treadmills had been used by two prisoners to grind corn or raise water from the ground, but this was something entirely new. The Discipline Mill was designed to achieve absolutely nothing. It was a gruelling, yet ultimately pointless exercise in 'grinding air'.

The invention consisted of a large cylinder that contained 24 steps. Handrails were installed for each prisoner and partitions ensured that they could neither see nor speak to one another as they worked. By standing on each step, it forced the cylinder to turn. Some treadmills had a bell attached to them which rang every 150 seconds, indicating how many rotations had been achieved. Prisoners were expected to turn the mill for up to six hours per day with a five-minute break after every 15 minutes.

With the passing of The Prisons Act 1865, every male over the age of 16, sentenced to hard labour, was forced to spend a minimum of three months of his sentence on the treadmill. Whilst Reformists believed that labour of the first class would improve the prisoners' wellbeing, the inmates themselves knew all too well how dangerous the Everlasting Staircase could be.

Considering how little the inmates were given to eat, calories were soon burnt, causing dizziness and exhaustion. If the prisoners lost concentration, even for a moment, they could miss the next step, slip forward and crash into the stairs as they continued rising. Loss of teeth was a regular occurrence and the steps were splashed with blood more often than not.

Gradually, prison wardens realised the free energy they were wasting and treadmills were coupled to corn grinders and water pumps, making it a benefit for the local community but still an arduous task for the unfortunate prisoners themselves.

As time passed, Victorians came to see the treadmill as a cruel form of torture rather than a means of overcoming idleness and they were finally abolished in 1902.

> "PRISONERS WERE EXPECTED TO TURN THE MILL FOR UP TO SIX HOURS PER DAY WITH A FIVE-MINUTE BREAK AFTER EVERY 15 MINUTES"

The Everlasting Staircase

Brixton prison treadmill was one of the largest and most feared of the Victorian age. It allowed only minimal rest for every hour's labour

Sir William Cubitt invented the first penal treadmill in 1817 after being angered by prisoners' "idleness"

Oscar Wilde died at age 46, two years after walking the treadmill at Pentonville Prison. He never recovered from the gruelling experience

Industry & Invention

THE CRYSTAL PALACE

London, UK
1851 – 1936

One of the most iconic and groundbreaking buildings of the Victorian era was undoubtedly the Crystal Palace. Erected in 1851 in Hyde Park, London, the impressive structure was designed by architect Joseph Paxton to house the Great Exhibition. The design of the Crystal Palace as one huge glass construction was based on the greenhouses that Paxton had previously designed and built for the Duke of Devonshire at Chatsworth House, Derbyshire. When Paxton's designs were officially accepted by the building committee of the Royal Commission on 15 July 1850, the construction of the Crystal Palace was set in motion.

The Great Exhibition of the Works of Industry of All Nations (to give the event its full name) was intended to be an international event to display items from around the world in four categories: Raw Materials, Machinery and Mechanical Inventions, Manufactures and Sculpture and Fine Art. When the Exhibition was opened at the Crystal Palace on 1 May 1851, it became a hugely successful and popular venture that inspired a series of similar exhibitions across the globe, which would come to be known as the World's Fairs. Items on display during the six months of the exhibition's tenure included the Koh-i-Noor diamond, an early version of the fax machine and an 80-blade penknife.

Over six million people visited the Great Exhibition at the Crystal Palace, including famous and influential figures like Charles Darwin, Charlotte Brontë, Karl Marx and Charles Dickens. Upon the Exhibition's closure, the Crystal Palace was moved to Sydenham Hill after public uproar at the prospect of the building being demolished. The Crystal Palace, though in a different location, continued to symbolise Victorian innovation and greatness until it was destroyed by a fire on 30 November 1936. The memory of the Crystal Palace remains synonymous with the Victorian Age and is firmly entrenched in British history.

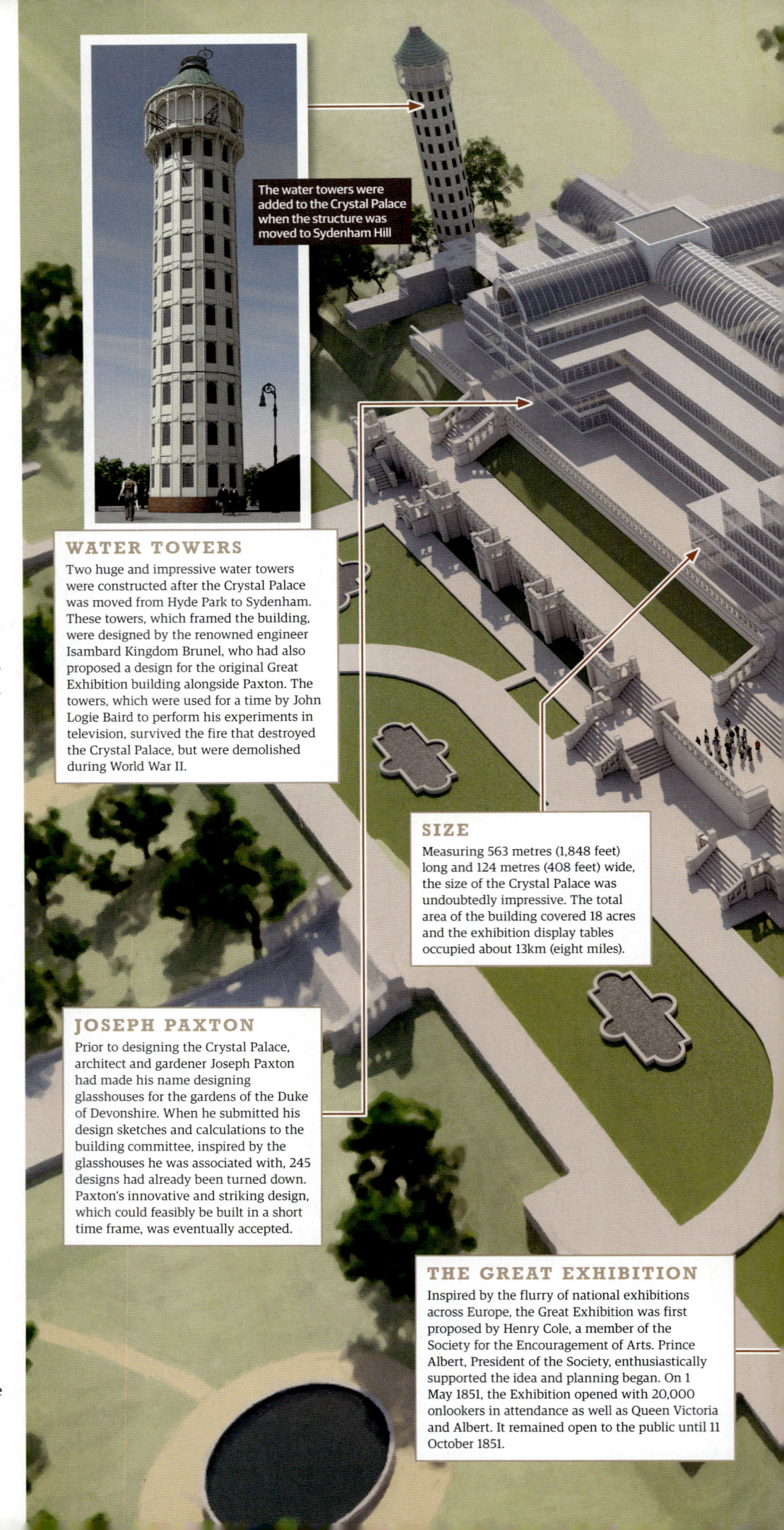

The water towers were added to the Crystal Palace when the structure was moved to Sydenham Hill

WATER TOWERS

Two huge and impressive water towers were constructed after the Crystal Palace was moved from Hyde Park to Sydenham. These towers, which framed the building, were designed by the renowned engineer Isambard Kingdom Brunel, who had also proposed a design for the original Great Exhibition building alongside Paxton. The towers, which were used for a time by John Logie Baird to perform his experiments in television, survived the fire that destroyed the Crystal Palace, but were demolished during World War II.

SIZE

Measuring 563 metres (1,848 feet) long and 124 metres (408 feet) wide, the size of the Crystal Palace was undoubtedly impressive. The total area of the building covered 18 acres and the exhibition display tables occupied about 13km (eight miles).

JOSEPH PAXTON

Prior to designing the Crystal Palace, architect and gardener Joseph Paxton had made his name designing glasshouses for the gardens of the Duke of Devonshire. When he submitted his design sketches and calculations to the building committee, inspired by the glasshouses he was associated with, 245 designs had already been turned down. Paxton's innovative and striking design, which could feasibly be built in a short time frame, was eventually accepted.

THE GREAT EXHIBITION

Inspired by the flurry of national exhibitions across Europe, the Great Exhibition was first proposed by Henry Cole, a member of the Society for the Encouragement of Arts. Prince Albert, President of the Society, enthusiastically supported the idea and planning began. On 1 May 1851, the Exhibition opened with 20,000 onlookers in attendance as well as Queen Victoria and Albert. It remained open to the public until 11 October 1851.

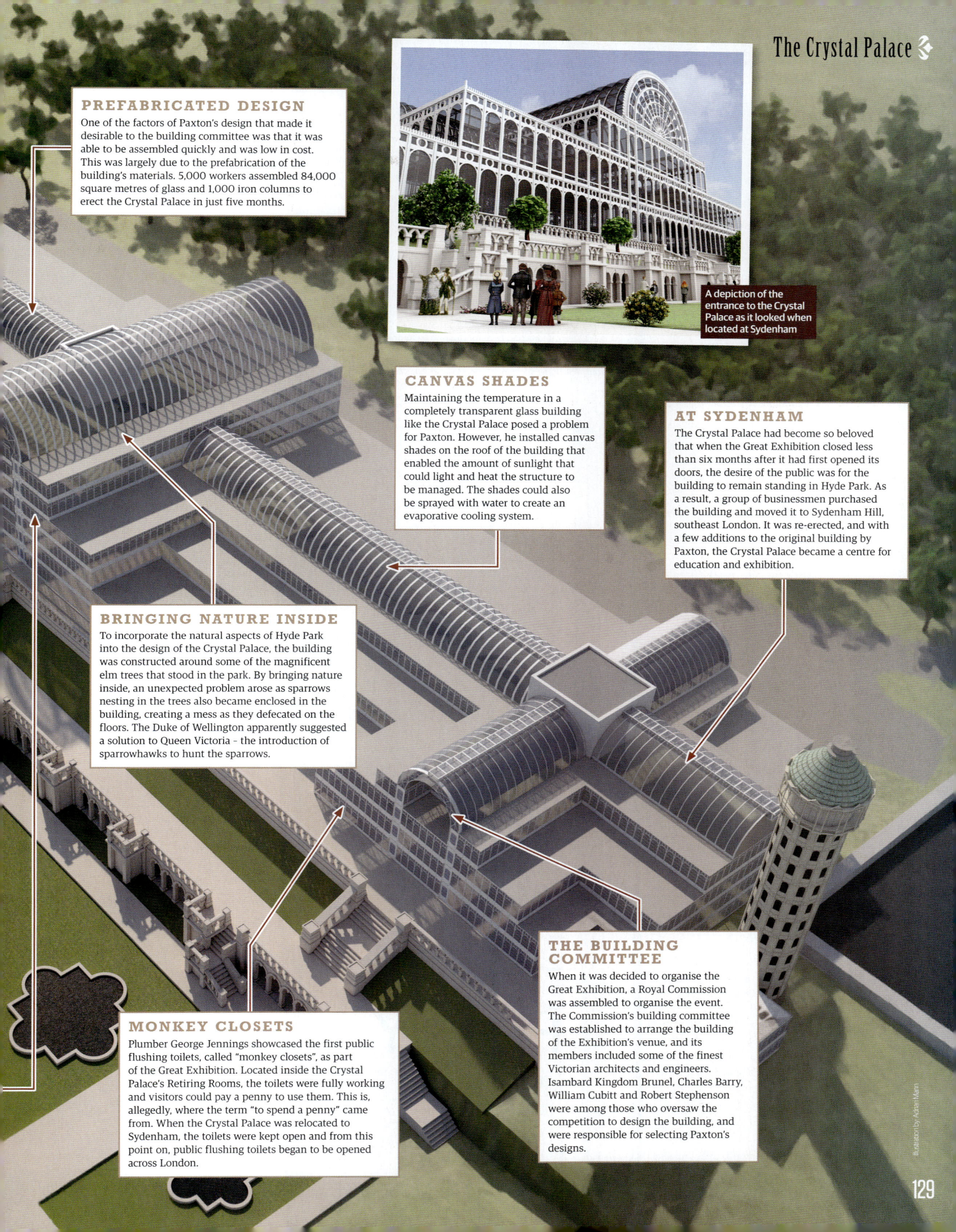

The Crystal Palace

PREFABRICATED DESIGN
One of the factors of Paxton's design that made it desirable to the building committee was that it was able to be assembled quickly and was low in cost. This was largely due to the prefabrication of the building's materials. 5,000 workers assembled 84,000 square metres of glass and 1,000 iron columns to erect the Crystal Palace in just five months.

A depiction of the entrance to the Crystal Palace as it looked when located at Sydenham

CANVAS SHADES
Maintaining the temperature in a completely transparent glass building like the Crystal Palace posed a problem for Paxton. However, he installed canvas shades on the roof of the building that enabled the amount of sunlight that could light and heat the structure to be managed. The shades could also be sprayed with water to create an evaporative cooling system.

AT SYDENHAM
The Crystal Palace had become so beloved that when the Great Exhibition closed less than six months after it had first opened its doors, the desire of the public was for the building to remain standing in Hyde Park. As a result, a group of businessmen purchased the building and moved it to Sydenham Hill, southeast London. It was re-erected, and with a few additions to the original building by Paxton, the Crystal Palace became a centre for education and exhibition.

BRINGING NATURE INSIDE
To incorporate the natural aspects of Hyde Park into the design of the Crystal Palace, the building was constructed around some of the magnificent elm trees that stood in the park. By bringing nature inside, an unexpected problem arose as sparrows nesting in the trees also became enclosed in the building, creating a mess as they defecated on the floors. The Duke of Wellington apparently suggested a solution to Queen Victoria - the introduction of sparrowhawks to hunt the sparrows.

THE BUILDING COMMITTEE
When it was decided to organise the Great Exhibition, a Royal Commission was assembled to organise the event. The Commission's building committee was established to arrange the building of the Exhibition's venue, and its members included some of the finest Victorian architects and engineers. Isambard Kingdom Brunel, Charles Barry, William Cubitt and Robert Stephenson were among those who oversaw the competition to design the building, and were responsible for selecting Paxton's designs.

MONKEY CLOSETS
Plumber George Jennings showcased the first public flushing toilets, called "monkey closets", as part of the Great Exhibition. Located inside the Crystal Palace's Retiring Rooms, the toilets were fully working and visitors could pay a penny to use them. This is, allegedly, where the term "to spend a penny" came from. When the Crystal Palace was relocated to Sydenham, the toilets were kept open and from this point on, public flushing toilets began to be opened across London.

Weird History of the Victorians

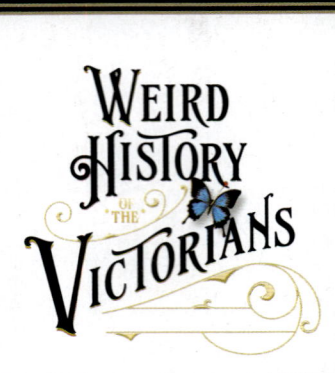

Future PLC Quay House, The Ambury, Bath, BA1 1UA

Editorial
Editor **April Madden**
Senior Art Editor **Andy Downes**
Head of Art & Design **Greg Whitaker**
Editorial Director **Jon White**
Managing Director **Grainne McKenna**

Contributors
Edoardo Albert, Ben Biggs, Melanie Clegg, Catherine Curzon, Nell Darby, Joanna Elphick, Ben Gazur, Bee Ginger, Philippa Grafton, Jack Griffiths, James Hoare, Callum McKelvie, Alice Pattillo and David Williamson

Cover images
Getty, Alamy, Adobe Stock

Photography
All copyrights and trademarks are recognised and respected

Advertising
Media packs are available on request
Commercial Director **Clare Dove**

International
Head of Print Licensing **Rachel Shaw**
licensing@futurenet.com
www.futurecontenthub.com

Circulation
Head of Newstrade **Tim Mathers**

Production
Head of Production **Mark Constance**
Production Project Manager **Matthew Eglinton**
Advertising Production Manager **Joanne Crosby**
Digital Editions Controller **Jason Hudson**
Production Managers **Keely Miller, Nola Cokely, Vivienne Calvert, Fran Twentyman**

Printed in the UK

Distributed by
Marketforce – www.marketforce.co.uk
For enquiries, please email: mfcommunications@futurenet.com

GPSR EU RP (for authorities only)
eucomply OÜ Pärnu mnt 139b-14 11317, Tallinn, Estonia
hello@eucompliancepartner.com, +3375690241

Weird History of the Victorians 01E Edition (AHB7026)
© 2025 Future Publishing Limited

We are committed to only using magazine paper which is derived from responsibly managed, certified forestry and chlorine-free manufacture. The paper in this bookazine was sourced and produced from sustainable managed forests, conforming to strict environmental and socioeconomic standards.

All contents © 2025 Future Publishing Limited or published under licence. All rights reserved. No part of this magazine may be used, stored, transmitted or reproduced in any way without the prior written permission of the publisher. Future Publishing Limited (company number 2008885) is registered in England and Wales. Registered office: Quay House, The Ambury, Bath BA1 1UA. All information contained in this publication is for information only and is, as far as we are aware, correct at the time of going to press. Future cannot accept any responsibility for errors or inaccuracies in such information. You are advised to contact manufacturers and retailers directly with regard to the price of products/services referred to in this publication. Apps and websites mentioned in this publication are not under our control. We are not responsible for their contents or any other changes or updates to them. This magazine is fully independent and not affiliated in any way with the companies mentioned herein.

FUTURE Connectors. Creators. Experience Makers.

Future plc is a public company quoted on the London Stock Exchange (symbol: FUTR)
www.futureplc.com

Chief Executive Officer **Kevin Li Ying**
Non-Executive Chairman **Richard Huntingford**
Chief Financial Officer **Sharjeel Suleman**

Tel +44 (0)1225 442 244

Part of the **ALL ABOUT HISTORY** bookazine series